D0518487

THIS BOOK BELONGS TO

....

To Mum & Dad; your love of nature is always inspiring.

E.J.

To Felix and Minkie who love the Great Outdoors as much as I do.

A.W.

First published 2019 by Nosy Crow Ltd.
The Crow's Nest, 14 Baden Place, Crosby Row
London SE1 1YW
www.nosycrow.com

ISBN 978 1 78800 482 4

A CIP catalogue record for this book is available from the British Library.

Printed in China

Papers used by Nosy Crow are made from wood grown in sustainable forests.

1 3 5 7 9 8 6 4 2

2020 NATURE MONTH-BY-MONTH

A Children's Almanac

Anna Wilson   Elly Jahnz

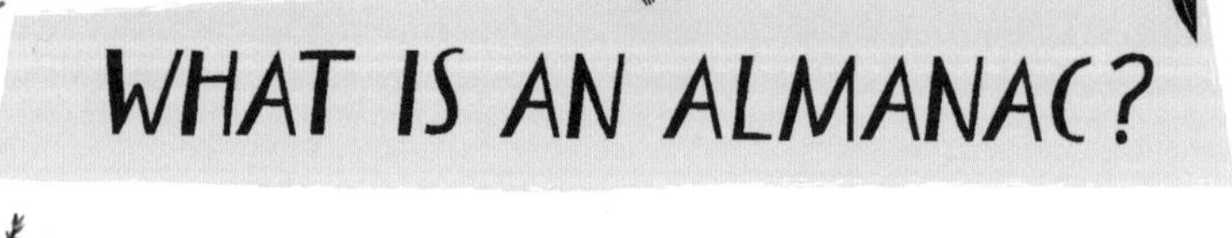

WHAT IS AN ALMANAC?

The first almanacs were created about 3,000 years ago! They were written by the ancient Egyptians who used a kind of paper made from reeds known as papyrus. The writers listed all the dates that were thought to be lucky or unlucky, and made predictions about the weather. Farmers used these almanacs to help them know when to plant seeds and when to harvest crops.

Nowadays you can also find almanacs (like this one!) which have fun facts about each month – things to do indoors and outdoors, animals to spot, festivals to celebrate and seasonal food to grow, cook and eat. They also contain information about the weather, the night sky and all sorts of other amazing facts.

WARNING!

This book contains activities which involve things like knives, saws, hammers and nails and hot ovens. There are also a lot of fun things to do outside which involve fire and very cold water! All the activities are safe if you are sensible, follow safety guidelines and take a grown-up along to look out for you.

CONTENTS

January 6-19

February 20-33

March 34-47

April 48-61

May 62-75

June 76-89

July 90-103

August 104-117

September 118-131

October 132-145

November 146-159

December 160-173

Calendar 174-179

Notes 180-185

Glossary 186-189

Index 190-192

JANUARY
SPECIAL DAYS
1st New Year's Day/First Footing
5th Twelfth Night/Wassailing
6th Epiphany
13th Lohri (Punjabi midwinter festival)
25th Chinese New Year/Burns Night

ANNIVERSARIES

125 years ago . . .

On 12 January 1895, the National Trust was set up by Octavia Hill, Sir Robert Hunter and Canon Hardwicke Rawnsley. These people thought it was important that Britain took care of its historic buildings and places of natural beauty, opening them for everyone to enjoy.

200 years ago . . .

On 17 January 1820, the writer Anne Brontë was born. She lived in Yorkshire and was famous for writing a book called *The Tenant of Wildfell Hall*. Her two sisters, Charlotte and Emily, were also writers.

"The blackest month of the year is the month of Janiveer."

People often talk about January as though it is the worst of all the months.

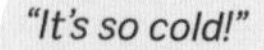

It's true that we don't see much daylight at this time of year. But wherever you live, you'll be able to find lots of things to get excited about in January. Yes, it's cold outside, but if you wrap up warm you can still enjoy walks and games and activities in the garden or park – or even by the sea. There are also some wonderful festivals in January which celebrate looking forward with hope to the year to come. So January's not that bad after all!

Why is January Called January?

The calendar we use today was invented by the Romans. January was named after the Roman god Janus who was the god of gates and doorways. He was always drawn with two faces looking in opposite directions – one face looked back at the year that had passed, and the other looked forwards into the new year.

DID YOU KNOW...

The Anglo-Saxons called January *Wulfmonath* because it was the month when hungry wolves prowled around, looking for food.

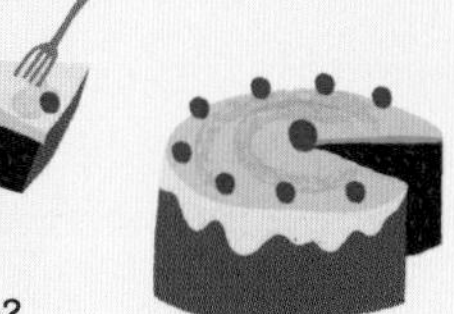

New Year's Resolutions

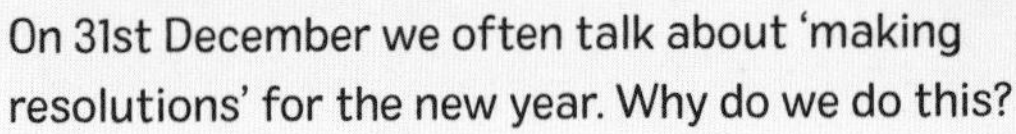

On 31st December we often talk about 'making resolutions' for the new year. Why do we do this?

The tradition of making resolutions started with the Romans, too. Because the January god, Janus, was looking backwards and forwards at the same time, he became a symbol for the Romans of forgetting what had happened in the past and moving on into the future. January therefore became known as a month in which to forgive people and be kind.

Nowadays people seem to worry more about getting fit and not eating chocolate – maybe we should be more like the Romans and make resolutions to be kinder instead?

Here are some ideas for resolutions that you might manage to keep . . .

- Look out for someone at school who needs a friend.
- Have a cake sale or organise a sponsored silence or a sponsored walk for charity.
- Clear out your old toys and clothes and take them to a charity shop. (Check with an adult before you give these things away!)
- Help out around the house and/or garden, if you have one.

FESTIVAL FUN

The colourful festivals of light such as Christmas, Hanukkah and Diwali might be over, but January has its fair share of celebrations to look forward to.

5th January *Twelfth Night*

For Christians, Twelfth Night used to be the day when Christmas was celebrated. In some countries, 6th January is still the day on which children get their presents. It is also known as Epiphany, St Nicholas's Day and the Feast of the Three Kings.

5th January *Wassailing*

Wassailing is a pagan tradition. The word *wassail* comes from the Anglo-Saxon words *waes hael* which mean 'good health'. The festival looks forward to what people hope for in the new year to come: good weather, good health and a good harvest.

Wassailing involves going out into the countryside to bless the apple trees. The wassail king and queen lead everyone in a sing-song around the tree to encourage it to produce lots of apples.

13th January *Lohri*

Hindus and Sikhs all over the world celebrate Lohri. During Lohri, songs are sung to the sun god, Surya, thanking him for his warmth and praying for his return after the cold weather.

People drink *gurh* – a delicious sugary drink made from sugarcane. *Gajak* is also eaten – a thin, dry sweet made from roasted sesame seeds cooked in sugar syrup and spices. Children go from house to house singing folk songs and are given sweets. In the evening, a bonfire is lit and people gather together to dance.

Recipe for *Twelfth Night Cake*

Whoever finds the bean hidden in the cake is king or queen for the evening. If you have saved a paper crown from your Christmas crackers, the king or queen can wear it!

You will need:

Large bowl
Electric whisk
Rolling pin
23 cm cake tin
Baking sheet
Greaseproof paper
Blunt knife
Wire rack

100 g butter, softened
100 g caster sugar
2 eggs (one whole, one yolk only)
100 g ground almonds
500 g puff pastry (you can buy this ready-made)
1 dried bean

To decorate: another egg, beaten, icing sugar

Be careful not to choke on the dried bean!

1. *Preheat the oven to 200°C/180°C fan/Gas Mark 6.*
2. *Mix the butter and sugar together with the electric whisk until it becomes pale and fluffy.*
3. *Beat in the eggs and then add the ground almonds.*
4. *Roll out half of the pastry until it is 3 mm thick.*
5. *Put the cake tin on top of the rolled-out pastry and cut around it with a blunt knife. Do the same with the other half.*
6. *Put the first circle on a baking sheet lined with greaseproof paper. Spread it with the almond filling and put the dried bean in somewhere, then put the second circle on the top.*
7. *Brush the top with beaten egg and use the knife to make a light criss-cross pattern.*
8. *Bake for 30 minutes. Take out and cool on the wire rack before dusting with icing sugar.*

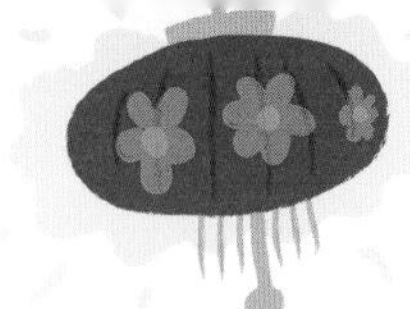

25th January *Chinese New Year*

This year, Chinese people all over the world will be celebrating the Year of the Rat. The rat is the first and the bravest of all the 12 animals of the Chinese Zodiac. Being born in the Year of the Rat is therefore regarded as an honour and a privilege, so if your family has a new baby in 2020, you are very lucky! Chinese New Year is a noisy and colourful occasion and there will be festivities in big cities throughout the UK. There are firecrackers, lion and dragon dances, music, parades, lanterns and special foods such as noodles. People wear red clothes for luck and to ward off evil spirits.

DID YOU KNOW...

The Rat of 2020 is the Gold Rat. People born under this sign are believed to be clever, talented, easily angered and jealous. Their lucky numbers are two and three and their lucky flowers are the lily and the African violet.

Recipe for *Sesame Noodles*

Serves 4. You can add other things to this recipe such as cooked chicken and cooked prawns if you like.

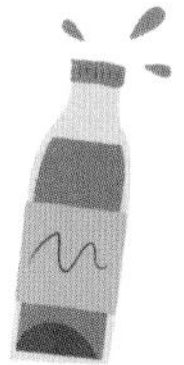

You will need:

Whisk	**4 tablespoons of dark soy sauce**
Small bowl	**2 cloves of garlic, finely sliced or crushed**
Saucepan	**2 tablespoons of rice vinegar**
Sieve	**3 tablespoons of sesame oil**
Chopsticks	**Splash of chilli oil or a pinch of dried red chillies**
	4 spring onions (scallions), finely sliced
	300 g thin dried egg noodles

1. *Whisk together the soy sauce, garlic, rice vinegar and oils.*
2. *Prepare the egg noodles following the instructions on the packet.*
3. *Pour the sauce over the warm noodles, top with spring onions and eat straight away!*

If you are not used to using chopsticks, have a go:

Step 1:

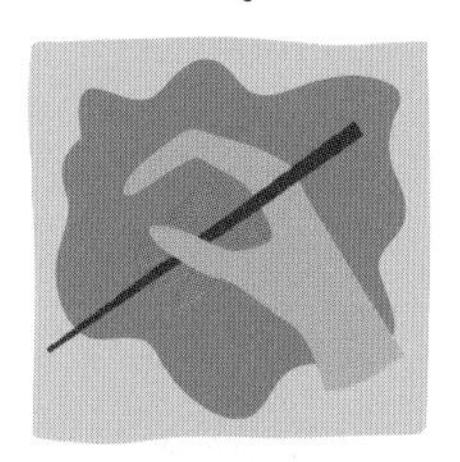

Hold the upper chopstick like a pencil, about one-third of the way from the top.

Step 2:

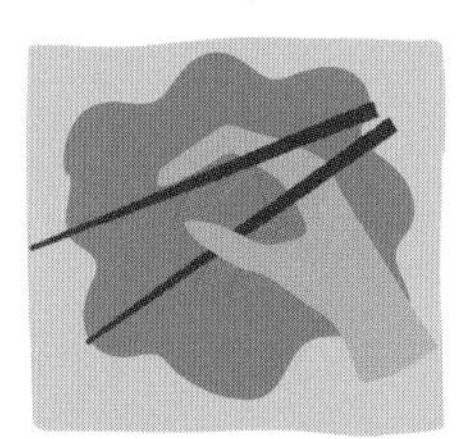

Place the second chopstick against your fourth finger and hold it in place with your thumb.

Step 3:

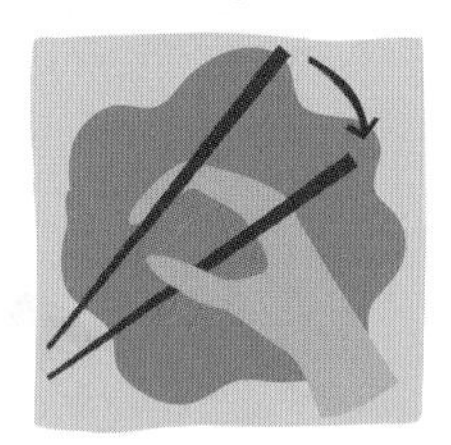

Move the upper chopstick with your thumb, first and middle fingers.

OUTDOOR ADVENTURES

It can be very hard to get up in the mornings in January. The sun doesn't seem to appear until school has begun – if it appears at all! But the dark mornings can be an exciting time for spotting wildlife. Even if you are not lucky enough to see an animal or bird, you might hear one instead if you listen hard.

Owls become very noisy at this time of year. You might catch sight of the large, silent shape of a tawny owl or a barn owl flying past you on your way to school.

Foxes and badgers are busy at this time of year, too. They have to work hard to find food to keep them alive through the cold winter. Sometimes you can see them knocking over rubbish bins in their search for food!

If you go out into the garden, the park or the woods near where you live, you will see signs of new life even on the darkest day. In colder northern regions, plants take longer to appear, while down in the south you might see daffodils as early as 1st January.

Snowdrops are already in bloom in January. Their tiny white and green heads look so delicate, but they are strong enough to survive the coldest weather – even snow and ice!

Other plants are quietly peeping out of the damp, dark ground, too. Hazel catkins can be seen hanging from the trees, even before the leaves start to show their shoots. Sometimes little yellow primroses start to appear now.

How to Make a *Nature Notebook*

1 *Take some sheets of scrap paper, fold them in half to make a booklet, then staple them together where you've made the fold.*

2 *Remember to make the notebook small enough to fit into a pocket so that you can take it with you wherever you go.*

3 *Tie a piece of string to a pencil and stick the loose end of the string into the notebook with sticky tape or make a hole in the pages and thread the string through. Use the pencil to note down where and when you see things while you are out and about.*

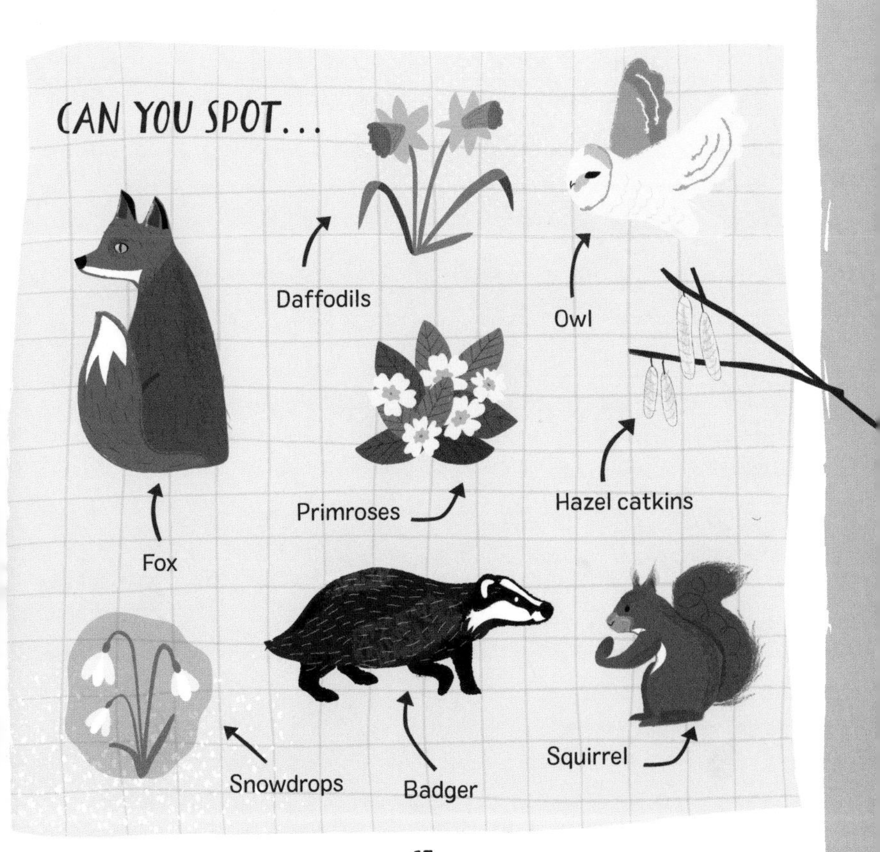

BIRD SPOTTING

The RSPB holds a survey called The Big Garden Birdwatch at the end of January every year. This is to encourage people to record the different types of birds that regularly visit our gardens and streets so that we can keep an eye on their habits and see how the weather has affected them. More than half a million people get involved every year. Check the RSPB website to see how you can get involved. **www.rspb.org.uk**

CAN YOU SPOT...

GREEN FINGERS IN WINTER

The garden might seem empty and bleak in January, but there are still things you can do to get ready for spring. Maybe this will be the year that you have a go at growing your own vegetables? You don't need a garden to do this – you can grow things in pots or 'grow bags' which you can buy from garden centres or DIY shops.

Potatoes are a good vegetable to start with. In January you can buy potatoes to 'chit'. These are potatoes with shoots growing from them which will eventually grow into new potato plants. These small shoots need light and a cool temperature (about 4°C) to start them off.

Stand the potatoes in egg boxes on a windowsill in a cool room or garden shed, making sure that the ends with the most shoots are facing upwards. After about 4–6 weeks, the potatoes will have grown quite a bit. Wait until the shoots have grown to about 3 cm long and then you can plant them in the earth when the weather is warmer in March or April.

You can also plant a tree in January. How about asking your school if you could plant an apple tree? Or even start a small vegetable garden, beginning with those potatoes?

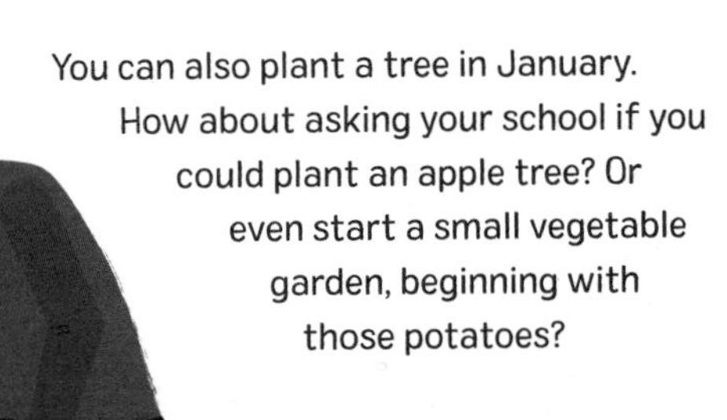

THE NIGHT SKY

If there are no clouds, January is a great time for stargazing. As it gets dark so early, you can wrap up warm and go outside to look at the night sky.

Sometimes we see only part of the moon, depending on where the moon is in its journey across the sky. The different stages of this journey are called the 'phases of the moon'.

Phases of the Moon in January 2020

Full Moon
10th January

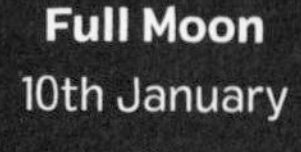

Last Quarter
17th January

First Quarter
3rd January

New Moon
24th January

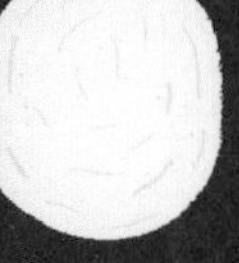

The full moon in January is known as the Wolf Moon.

WINTER WALKS

It is tempting not to go outside at all in January if you can help it! However, often it's better to be out in the cold than to be inside staring miserably at it through the window.

'Poohsticks' is a good game for this time of year as the rivers and streams are usually quite high and so the water is flowing fast.

Poohsticks

This game comes from the lovely stories of the bear Winnie-the-Pooh by A. A. Milne. Pooh plays the game with his friends Christopher Robin and Piglet.

1. *First, you need to find a narrow bridge over a stream or river. Then you need to find a small stick for each person who wants to play.*
2. *Line up along the bridge, facing the flow of the river – in other words, the water should be flowing towards you and running under the bridge away from you.*
3. *Hold your sticks over the edge. Be very careful not to lean too far!*
4. *Choose one person to be the judge – they must say, "Ready, steady, go!" and then everyone drops their stick straight down into the river. Do not cheat by throwing your stick under the bridge!*
5. *Run to the other side of the bridge and watch the sticks come out. The first one to appear is the winner!*

SPECIAL DAYS

1st Imbolc (pagan celebration)

2nd Candlemas (Christian festival)

10th Tu B'Shevat (Jewish New Year)

14th St Valentine's Day

25th Shrove Tuesday (Pancake Day)

26th Ash Wednesday (Christian festival)

29th Leap day

ANNIVERSARIES

75 years ago . . .

On 6 February 1945, the Jamaican musician Bob Marley was born. He is famous for writing and singing reggae music, and his album *Legend* is the bestselling reggae album of all time.

80 years ago . . .

On 10 February 1940, the first cartoon of Tom and Jerry was made by William Hanna and Joseph Barbera.

200 years ago . . .

On 28 February 1820, the illustrator John Tenniel was born. He is most famous for his illustrations for *Alice's Adventures in Wonderland* and *Through the Looking-Glass*, written by Lewis Carroll.

"Surely as cometh the winter, I know there are spring violets under the snow."

R. H. NEWELL (1836–1901)

February starts off cold and dark – at first it seems even more wintery than January! But by the end of the month we will have two hours more daylight and spring will be around the corner.

People often think of February as a time to be quiet and thoughtful before nature wakes up from its long winter's sleep. A few religions hold a 'fast' during this month, which means that people do not eat anything during daylight hours. Some Christians fast during Lent, which often occurs in February. Buddhists fast during a full moon. Some pagans fast in preparation for Ostara, the spring festival. The idea is that fasting helps you to clear your mind and focus on prayer.

By the middle of February, we can feel tired and in need of a break – so it's a good thing that the half-term holidays happen this month!

Why is February Called February?

The Latin name for this month was *Februarius*. It came from the Latin word *februum* which means 'purification'. The Romans thought of the 5th day of this month as the official first day of spring. On the 15th they celebrated a festival called *Februa*.

This was a time to get rid of evil spirits and to cleanse the air so that people felt fit and healthy for spring. This is where we get our idea of spring cleaning from. Perhaps you could use the colder, darker days this month to tidy your bedroom or help clear out the shed or garage.

FEBRUARY BIRTH SIGNS

Aquarius

The sign of the water-carrier. Some people believe that if you have your birthday between 20th January and 18th February, then this is your sign. You are supposed to be an inquisitive and logical person who does not like to follow rules just for the sake of it.

Pisces

This is the sign of the fish. If you are born between 19th February and 20th March, then you are a Piscean. Some people believe this means you are very emotional, creative and good at working out things based on your feelings.

DID YOU KNOW...

Before the Romans changed the calendar, the length of February used to change a lot. At one point it had only 23 days. The Anglo-Saxons called February *Solmonath*, which means 'the month of cakes'. This is because cakes and bread were offered to the gods to make sure that there would be a good harvest that year.

FESTIVAL FUN

February is not all about fasting, cleaning and staying quiet. There are lots of celebrations happening all around the world, too. Some have serious meanings, but others are good fun!

1st February *Imbolc*

Imbolc (pronounced 'imulk') is a pagan festival. Its name comes from the Celtic word *imbolg* which means 'in the belly'. This is because nature seems to be expecting lots of babies at this time of year – baby animals, baby trees, baby flowers and fruit and vegetables. Everything is hidden away at the moment, but that doesn't mean nothing is happening deep in the cold, dark ground – or inside pregnant animals! To celebrate, people sometimes make dolls made of corn called 'Bridey Dolls' which are said to bring good luck.

2nd February *Candlemas*

Candlemas is a Christian festival. It celebrates the day that the baby Jesus was taken to the temple for the first time. The festival always takes place on 2nd February and marks the end of the Christmas season. At Ripon Cathedral in Yorkshire, people celebrate by lighting 5,000 candles to symbolise Jesus bringing light into the darkness of the world.

14th February *St Valentine's Day*

St Valentine's Day is an ancient tradition. Today, it's seen as a day to celebrate love. People send cards and flowers (particularly red roses), chocolates and other gifts. In some parts of Norfolk and Suffolk there is an old custom of leaving presents on people's doorsteps on St Valentine's Eve, the night before St Valentine's Day.

25th February *Shrove Tuesday (Pancake Day)*

Shrove Tuesday gets its name from the ancient Christian practice of being 'shriven', which means being forgiven for things you've done wrong. It was traditional to tell a priest about anything bad you had done to get it out of the way before Lent, the season of fasting. Then, during the fast, you could concentrate on asking for forgiveness and promising to live a better life. On Shrove Tuesday, people used up eggs and fatty foods because during Lent they were not allowed to eat these things. One of the best ways of using up eggs and fat is to make pancakes, and a lot of people still do this today. That is why we also call this day Pancake Day.

26th February *Ash Wednesday*

Ash Wednesday is the first day of Lent. After all the pancake-eating and feasting, it is a quieter, more serious day. Christians spend the time thinking about how to live a better life and looking forward to Easter. Some go to church and the priest or vicar draws a cross on their foreheads in ash. This is to remember that Jesus died on the cross to save them from the things they had done wrong.

Recipe for *Blueberry Pancakes*

You will need:

Large mixing bowl
Small bowl or glass jug
Whisk
Wooden spoon
Non-stick frying pan
Tablespoon
Spatula
Serving plate
Kitchen paper or a clean tea towel

200 g self-raising flour
1 teaspoon of baking powder
Pinch of salt
1 egg
300 ml full fat milk
Small knob of butter
150 g fresh blueberries
Sunflower oil or a little butter for frying
Golden or maple syrup

1 *Mix the flour, baking powder and salt in the large bowl.*

2 *Beat the egg with the milk in the smaller bowl or jug.*

3 *Whisk the wet ingredients in until you have a thick, smooth batter.*

4 *Beat the small knob of butter into the milk and egg mixture.*

5 *Gently stir in half of the blueberries.*

6 *Heat a teaspoon of oil or a small amount of butter in the frying pan over a medium heat.*

7 *Drop a large tablespoon of the batter into the pan to make a pancake about 7 cm wide. If your pan is large enough, you can cook more than one pancake at a time, but don't let them touch.*

8 *Cook for about three minutes until small bubbles start to appear on the top of each pancake, then turn them with the spatula and cook the other side for another three minutes until golden.*

9 *Transfer to a serving plate and cover with kitchen paper or a tea towel to keep the pancakes warm while you make more.*

10 *Serve with golden or maple syrup and the rest of the blueberries.*

WEATHER

"When halo rings moon or Sun,
Rain's approaching on the run."

This is an old country saying, and there is some truth in it. If you see a halo around the moon or sun at this time of year, it is because ice crystals can sometimes form in high clouds. These make a ring or 'halo' appear, and later these crystals may fall as rain. Rainy days can seem boring, but remember that the rain is doing a good job of watering all those tiny plants that are waiting for spring to arrive. Also, the rain comes from clouds which come in all shapes and sizes. Cloud spotting can be fun – what kind of pictures and shapes can you see in the clouds today?

Cloud Spotting

Most of our names for clouds come from Latin. They are a combination of the following:

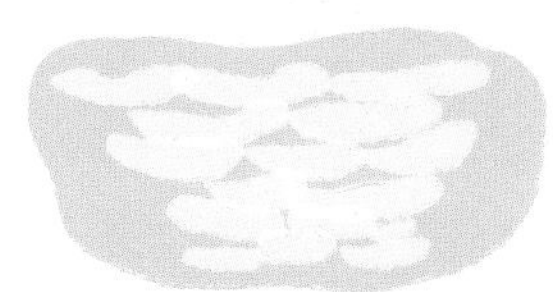

Stratus/strato =
low, flat/layered and smooth

Cumulus/cumulo =
heaped up/puffy, like cauliflower

Cirrus/cirro =
High up/wispy

Alto =
Medium level

Nimbus/nimbo =
Rain-bearing cloud

Combining the names tells you a bit more about the clouds. For example: nimbus + stratus = 'nimbostratus'. This is a cloud which is flat and layered and will probably bring rain. 'Cumulonimbus' is a puffy cloud which will bring rain, too.

THE SOLAR SYSTEM

The sun is in the middle of the solar system – the Earth and all the planets listed below move around the sun, and the moon moves around the Earth.

Sun Mercury Venus Earth Mars Jupiter Saturn Uranus Neptune

Constellation of the Month

Canis Major, or the 'Great Dog', can be seen this month. It chases Orion, the 'Hunter', across the sky. To find it, look for Sirius, the 'Dog Star'. In fact, this is two stars very close together which is why it is so bright. It is one of the closest stars to planet Earth.

DID YOU KNOW...

You can actually see Mercury, Venus, Mars, Jupiter and Saturn with the naked eye, but they are so far away they look just like stars.

LEAP YEARS

2020 is known as a leap year because this year February has 29 days instead of the usual 28. This means that 2020 has 366 days instead of 365.

★ A leap year happens once every four years.
★ Julius Caesar decided we should have leap years. He realised that the Earth goes around the sun in 365 ¼ days, so he added up the quarters to make an extra day every four years!
★ The Olympics happen every leap year. This year they will be held in Tokyo, in Japan.
★ In the old days, there was a tradition that 29th February was the day when a woman could ask a man to marry her.
★ If the man said no, he had to buy the woman a silk dress or 12 pairs of gloves!
★ The story goes that St Brigid of Ireland started the tradition in the 1st century: she complained to St Patrick that it was wrong for women to have to wait for men to propose.
★ In Greece, it is believed to be bad luck to get married in a leap year.
★ People born on a leap day are often called 'leaplings' or 'leapers'.
★ There are 4 million leaplings or leapers in the world.
★ Most of them celebrate their birthday on 28th February or 1st March on non-leap years.

GREEN FINGERS IN WINTER

There are lots of tidying-up jobs to do outside at this time of year to get the garden ready: so it's all about spring cleaning!

If you have a pond, you need to make sure it doesn't freeze over, as fish won't be able to breathe. You can stop the surface of the pond turning to ice by putting a tennis ball in the water – or even a rubber duck!

You can also get planting for next year. Why not put some snowdrop bulbs in the ground or in pots? Maybe ask your school if you can plant some. Mint grows well in pots, too. It is delicious added to cooked peas or boiled new potatoes. Add it to a glass of iced sparkling water for a refreshing drink.

Feed the Birds

Small birds are hungry at this time of year. They need to eat all day to get enough food to keep them going through the winter. You can help by making your own treats for the birds using food scraps from home.

Recipe for *Fat Cakes*

Mix one cup of melted fat with two cups of dry food.
If you want to make more, just double or triple the quantities.

You will need:

Large mixing bowl
Medium-sized saucepan
Wooden spoon
Old yoghurt pots or large, dried, 'open' pine cones
Metal skewer
Garden string
Scissors
Washing-up gloves

Any of the following:
Sultanas
Porridge oats
Bread or cake crumbs
Grated cheese
Unsalted peanuts
Wild birdseed
Fat (lard or suet)

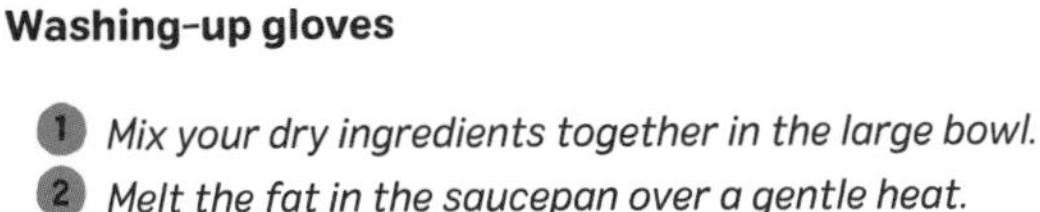

1. *Mix your dry ingredients together in the large bowl.*
2. *Melt the fat in the saucepan over a gentle heat.*
3. *Pour the melted fat over the dry ingredients.*
4. *Stir well until all the dry food is covered in the fat. Let it cool slightly while you prepare the yoghurt pot or pine cone.*
5. *If you are using a yoghurt pot, make a hole in the bottom of the pot using a metal skewer. Thread a piece of string through the hole. The string should be long enough for you to tie it to a bird table or branch of a tree. Make a knot in the bottom of the string.*
6. *Fill the pot with the warm food mix, squashing it down with your fingers (wearing gloves) so that the pot is filled right up.*
7. *Place the filled pots in the fridge overnight to set.*
8. *Next day, cut through the pot and carefully peel it away from the hardened fat mixture.*
9. *You now have a fat cake ready to hang on a tree or bird table!*

Pine cone variation:

1. *Make the food mix in the same way.*
2. *Tie a length of string securely around the stalk end of the cone.*
3. *Scoop up chunks of the warm food mix with your fingers (wearing gloves) and squash the mix into the gaps in the pine cone, packing it in as tightly as you can.*
4. *Leave in the fridge overnight to set.*
5. *Next day, take it out and hang it up for the birds!*

LET IT SNOW

Although we think of having a 'white Christmas', it's much more likely to snow in February in Britain. If it does this year, you won't have to think hard about the fun you can have outdoors. Everyone loves rushing out to make the first footprints in the snow, catching snowflakes on their tongue, having a snowball fight, sledging or building a snowman.

If you wrap up extra warm, you can make snow angels: lie down in a patch of freshly fallen snow and move your arms and legs up and down in the snow. Get up carefully and look at the pattern left behind – you've made a snow angel!

With a bit of help, you can also build a small igloo by packing the snow up into walls.

Or you can make snow bricks by using a spade to cut chunks of snow into cubes. Remember to leave a gap so that you can crawl inside.

You can also create wonderful snow lanterns by building a pyramid of snowballs and placing a tea light in the middle. Ask an adult to help you light the tea light and put it in the middle of your finished pile of snowballs.

WILDLIFE ON THE MOVE

Toads, frogs and newts are often on the move in February. They walk and hop a long way to find others to breed with. The females then go on another long journey back to their ponds. They follow the same route, year after year. This sometimes gets them into trouble, as they cross roads which were not there hundreds of years ago.

To help protect the amphibians from getting squashed, there are Toad Patrols up and down the country which go out in the evenings and pick the creatures up and carry them safely across the road. You can help amphibians to migrate safely by joining a patrol near you.

To find a Toad Crossing near you, go to **www.froglife.org** and follow the links. It's good fun and you can do some stargazing and wildlife-watching too as foxes, badgers and owls are out in the evening as well.

CAN YOU SPOT...

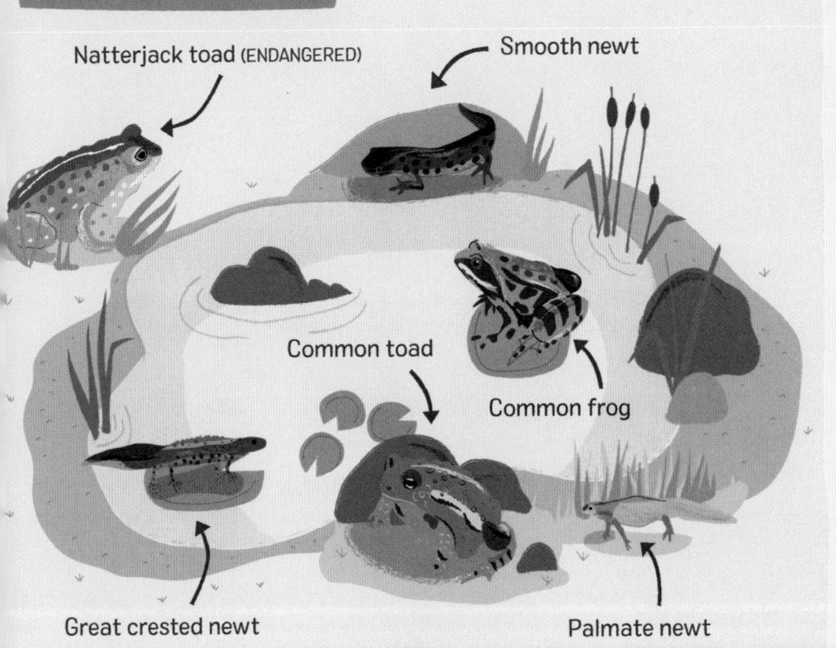

MARCH
SPECIAL DAYS
1st St David's Day (Wales)
5th St Piran's Day (Cornwall)
10th Holi (Hindu 'festival of colours')/ Purim (Jewish festival)
17th St Patrick's Day (Ireland)
20th Spring equinox (first day of spring)/Ostara (pagan celebration)
22nd Mother's Day/Isra and Mi'raj (Muslim celebration)
29th Daylight saving (clocks go forward)

ANNIVERSARIES

75 years ago . . .

12 March 1945
This is the day we remember a girl called Anne Frank who is believed to have died in March 1945 in the Nazi concentration camp of Bergen-Belsen. Her father, Otto Frank, published her diaries in 1947: he wanted the world to remember his daughter and never to forget the terrible things that happened to the Jewish people in the Second World War.

"March comes in like a lion,
and out like a lamb."

This saying describes how March can be quite cold and blustery to start with, but by the end of the month it feels as though spring is in the air at last! After 29th March this year we will have one extra hour of daylight, when the clocks go forward. There will be many more flowers to see, the birds will be singing their hearts out and the baby lambs will be jumping about in the fields.

DID YOU KNOW...

Every year March ends on the same day of the week as June.

Why is March Called March?

The Romans called this month *Martius*. It was named after the god of war and farming. That might seem a strange combination, but both war and farming began again in March after the long winter months. Even soldiers didn't like getting cold and wet! The Anglo-Saxons called March *Lentmonath*, which means 'lengthening month', because of the way that the daylight increases during this time. It is also where we get the word 'Lent' from.

Spring Equinox

20th March is the spring equinox. This is one of the days in the year in which the number of hours of daylight is exactly equal to the number of hours of darkness. This happens because the rays of the sun are shining straight at the equator (the middle of the Earth).

FESTIVAL FUN

10th March *Holi*

Holi is a Hindu festival also known as the 'festival of colours' or the 'festival of love', when Hindus celebrate the victory of good over evil and the arrival of spring. They meet to play and laugh, forget and forgive, and make up with people they have fallen out with! Holi lasts for a night and a day, starting on the evening of the *Purnima* (full moon day). People light bonfires and pray that evil will be destroyed. Then they smear each other with coloured paints and drench each other using water pistols and water-filled balloons! Imagine the world's biggest water fight out in the streets, and that is Holi! Everyone joins in: friend or stranger, rich or poor, man or woman, children or older people.

10th March *Purim*

Purim begins on the evening of 9th and ends on the evening of 10th March. It is a Jewish holiday during which Jewish people remember that long ago their people were saved from Haman, a cruel man who worked for the King of Persia. At Purim, people have a big feast and send money and gifts of food to people in need. It is a time to think of others and be thankful for a good life.

20th March *Ostara*

Ostara is a pagan festival which is celebrated at the spring equinox. For pagans, it's a time of year when everything in the natural world is in perfect balance because the day and the night are the same length. The festival takes its name from Ostara or Ēostre, the goddess of renewal and rebirth. She has the head of a hare. Because hares are nocturnal (awake at night and asleep in the day) they are closely linked with the moon, as both come out at night. Hares also represent the rebirth of nature in spring.

22nd March *Isra and Mi'raj*

This festival is in two parts. The first part, the *Isra* or the 'Night Journey', starts on the evening before the day of celebrations. Muslims remember the Prophet Muhammad's journey from Mecca to Jerusalem and then to heaven. Muslim people believe the Night Journey started when the Angel Gabriel took the Prophet Muhammad to Jerusalem on a winged horse, where he met and prayed with prophets including Moses and Jesus.

The second part is the *Mi'raj*, which means 'ladder' in Arabic. This was when the Prophet Muhammad was carried up to heaven by Gabriel where he spoke to Allah (God), who told the prophet that Muslims should say their prayers five times a day.

At Isra and Mi'raj, Muslim people say prayers during the night and Muslim cities keep their lights on all night.

Recipe for *Ostara Buns*

You will need:

Large mixing bowl
Baking tray
Greaseproof paper
Small bowl
Food mixer or wooden spoon
Piping bag and narrow nozzle
(and a very steady hand!)

Buns:
900 g plain white flour
450 g caster sugar
110 g butter or margarine
200 g marzipan or almond paste
½ teaspoon of baking powder
1 teaspoon of cinnamon
5 medium eggs, beaten

Icing:
225 g icing sugar
¼ teaspoon of almond extract
1 tablespoon of soft butter or margarine
4 teaspoons of water

1. *Preheat the oven to 180°C/160°C fan/Gas Mark 4.*
2. *Mix the bun ingredients in the large bowl using your hands until a medium-soft dough forms.*
3. *Add a little flour if the dough is too sticky.*
4. *Break off small chunks of dough, about 3 cm across, and roll them into balls.*
5. *Place the balls on a baking tray lined with greaseproof paper, making sure they are not too close together.*
6. *Press each ball slightly to flatten the top.*
7. *Bake until golden brown (about 15-20 minutes) then set aside to cool while you make the icing.*
8. *Beat the icing ingredients together in a food mixer or with a wooden spoon.*
9. *Put the nozzle in the narrow end of the piping bag and spoon the icing into the bag.*
10. *Hold the bag a few centimetres above each bun and squeeze out the icing to make a cross on top. If you don't have a piping bag add more water to the mixture and you can drizzle the icing on top using a spoon.*

22nd March *Mother's Day*

Mother's Day (or Mothering Sunday) always falls on the fourth Sunday in Lent, three weeks before Easter Day. It was originally a Christian festival, when people would go back to their 'mother' church if they had moved away from their home town. It has now become a day for people to say thank you to their mothers or carers. Why not make a card to show your mother or carer how much they mean to you?

Make a *Mother's Day Card*

You will need:

Piece of A6 white card
Some coloured paper in green, blue or pink
Yellow paper for daffodil petals
Orange paper for daffodil centre
Milk bottle top
PVC glue or a glue stick
Ruler
Scissors
Coloured pens or pencils

1. *Cut a rectangle of coloured paper that measures 1 cm less than your white card both length- and width-ways.*
2. *Stick the coloured paper on to the white card so that there is a white frame all the way around the colour.*
3. *Draw a petal shape on to the corner of the yellow paper – make it about 4 cm long.*
4. *Cut out five more petal shapes, using your first one as a template.*
5. *Fold your card in half and stick your petals in a flower shape around the middle of the crease.*
6. *Draw around the milk bottle top on a piece of orange paper.*
7. *Cut out your orange circle and stick it in the middle of the crease.*
8. *Use pens or pencils to write your message on the front of the card. You can decorate it with extra drawings, too!*

TOP TIP

To make your daffodil 'pop' out, make a tube of orange paper for the centre of the flower and stick it on top of the circle with sticky tape!

WAKEY-WAKEY!

Creatures such as hedgehogs, dormice, bumblebees, butterflies and bats come out of hibernation at this time of year. They wake up from a long winter's sleep and immediately go searching for food to fill their empty bellies.

Maybe you have a tortoise as a pet? If so, you'll need to wake him or her up around this time. Wait until the outside temperature is at least 10°C before you move your tortoise outside, though. It will be a bit of a shock, moving from a cosy hibernation box to the chilly garden or patio!

OUT AND ABOUT

There are more birds and animals to see in March. Some of them, such as chiffchaffs and wheatears, are visitors from other countries. It will depend where you live in the UK as to whether you are likely to see these birds. Some of them are found only in wetland areas or by the sea.

CAN YOU SPOT...

Chiffchaff

Sand martin

Sandwich tern

Blackcap

Chaffinch

Wheatear

Skylark

Lapwing

DID YOU KNOW...

Skylarks start singing before the sun rises, so their voice is the first to be heard in the dawn chorus. Sadly, the numbers of skylarks are falling in all European countries. It is thought that this is because farmers now sow their crops in autumn rather than in spring – this means that skylarks no longer have the habitat they need in which to breed and survive.

HOW TO BUILD A NEST BOX

If you are going to make a nest box, you should complete it and hang it up early in March so that it is ready for the birds to start making their nest inside.

Nest boxes should always be made from wood. Metal and plastic are not good materials to use as they may mean that the nest will overheat or get wet and this will harm the eggs and the chicks. It is important that the inside of the box doesn't get too cold either.

You will need:

- ★ **Short planks of strong wood, at least 15 mm thick (oak or beech is best as pine is rather soft and doesn't last as long)**
- ★ **Saw**
- ★ **Stainless steel nails (not glue – nails allow water to drain out of the box)**
- ★ **Hammer**
- ★ **Waterproof hinge for the lid (see page 45)**
- ★ **Helpful grown-up!**

Follow the diagram below:

Make sure your grown-up drills a few holes in the base of your box so that any rain that does get in can drain out quickly.

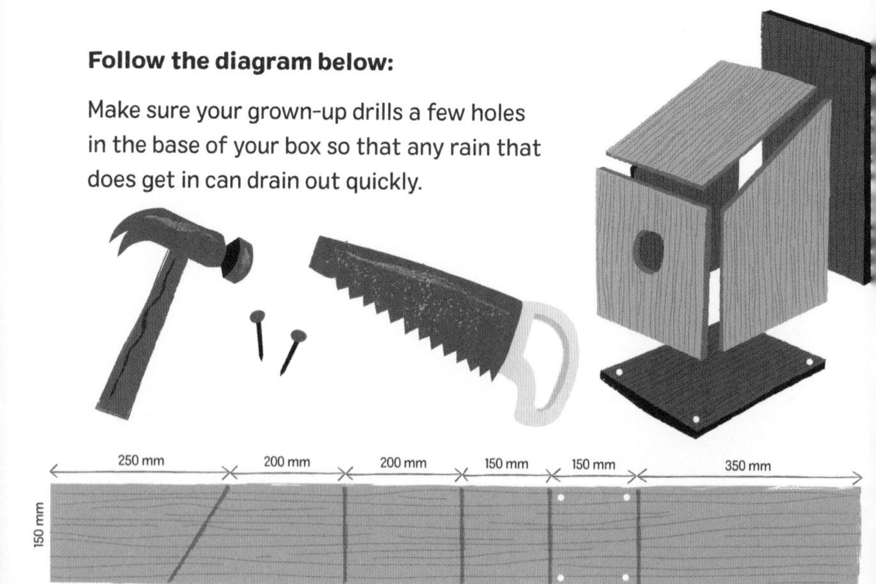

TOP TIP

The number of swifts is falling. Encourage them to visit by building a larger nest box (55 mm hole) and attaching it to the side of your house or high up in a tree!

Hole sizes

Different birds need different-sized holes:

- **25 mm** or larger for blue, coal and marsh tit;
- **28 mm** or larger for great tit and tree sparrow;
- **32 mm** for house sparrow.

Making a hinge

A lid is important so that you can get into the box easily to check what is going on inside – and to clean it each season. Attach a waterproof hinge to the roof of the box, so that it can be lifted easily but won't fall off. You can use pieces of tyre inner tubes or cut-up plastic milk bottles to make your hinge. Cut the rubber or plastic to the width of the box, and then nail it along the back of the box and to the roof.

DOWN BY THE RIVER

If you can get to a river, keep a sharp look-out for kingfishers. At this time of year the male bird is very busy, zipping along the surface of the water looking for fish – and a female to build a nest with!

CAN YOU SPOT...

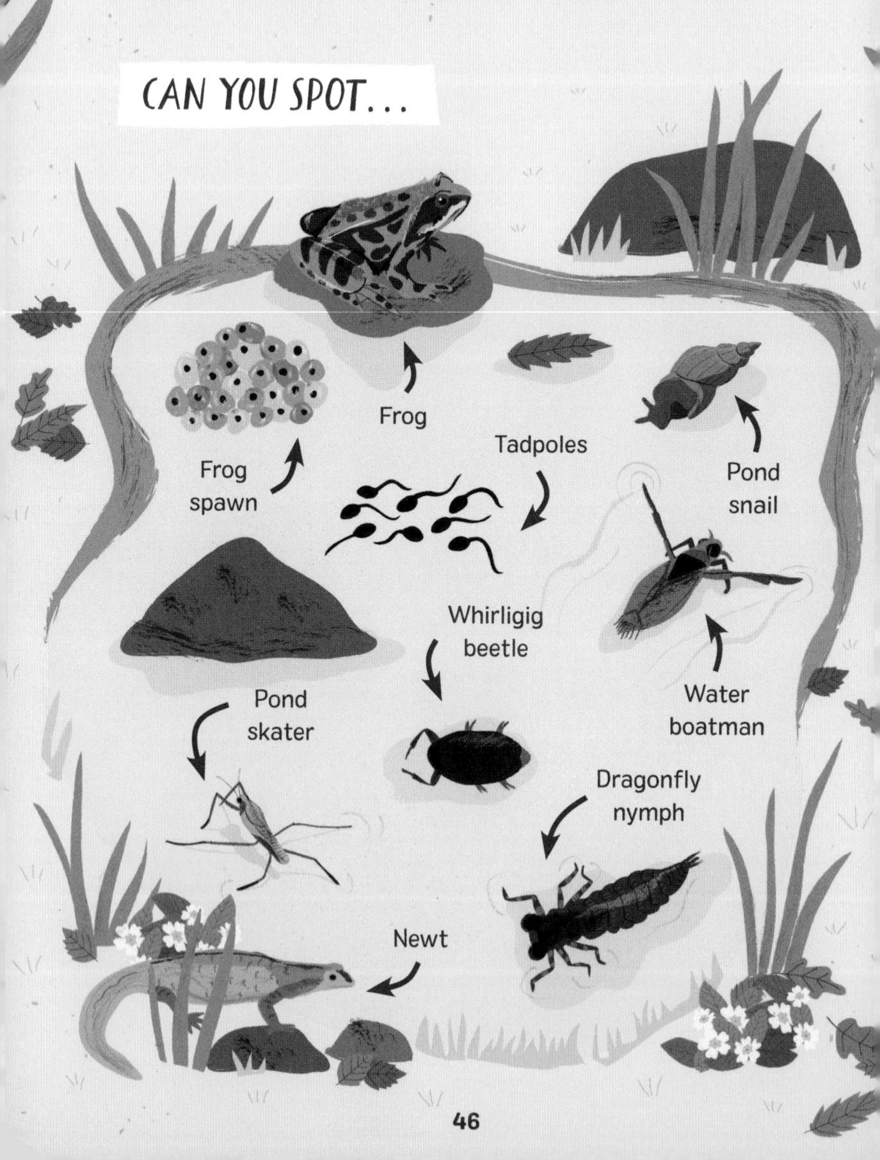

Pond Dipping

You don't need a garden pond to do this! Go for a walk to your nearest river or stream, or find a pond in a park. Make sure you wear wellies and warm waterproof clothing, and always go dipping with a grown-up.

You will need:

Fishing net
Container (bucket or tub)
Your nature notebook and pencil

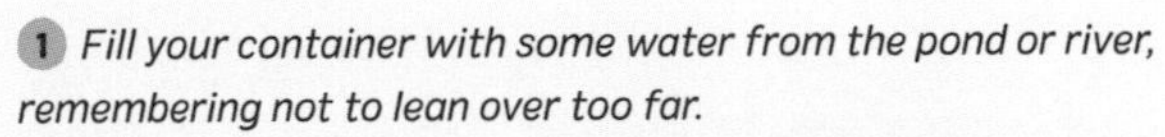

1. *Fill your container with some water from the pond or river, remembering not to lean over too far.*
2. *Place your container on the ground, a safe distance from the water's edge.*
3. *Dip your net into the water and swish it gently to and fro, then lift it out and tip it carefully into your container.*
4. *Note down what you've found in your nature notebook.*

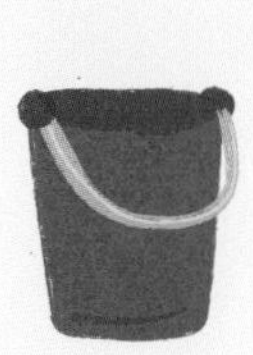

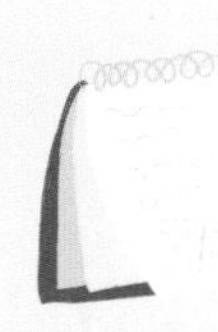

DID YOU KNOW...

Dragonflies have been around on Earth for about 300 million years. Some of the first species may have been the size of seagulls!

APRIL

SPECIAL DAYS

1st April Fool's Day

8th Passover begins (Jewish celebration)

12th Easter Sunday (Christian celebration)

23rd Ramadan begins (Muslim month of prayer and fasting)/St George's Day (England)/William Shakespeare's Birthday

ANNIVERSARIES

250 years ago . . .

On 7 April 1770, the English poet William Wordsworth was born. His poem 'I Wandered Lonely as a Cloud', written in 1804, is one of the most famous poems in the English language.

65 years ago . . .

On 18 April 1955, the famous scientist and mathematician Albert Einstein died. He is best known for his equation $E=mc^2$, which explained that even the smallest amount of mass (which is in everything on the planet!) can be turned into a huge amount of energy.

"Sweet April showers do spring May flowers."

THOMAS TUSSER (1524–1580)

People often moan about poor old April because it's a rainy month. One famous writer, T. S. Eliot, called it 'the cruellest month', but it actually has less rain in total than some other months. In any case, if we had no rain in April, those 'May flowers' would not 'spring' up!

It is true that April showers can be annoying. Those short, sharp bursts of rain seem to come from nowhere and disappear just as quickly. You have to remember to take an umbrella out with you in April even if the sun is shining when you leave the house! This is because the sky is full of cumulonimbus (those big, puffy white clouds) which burst into rain and then clear away again to leave blue sky.

It can still be very cold in the mornings, too – you might see frost on the grass early in the day. There can also be heavy snow in the hills. So basically, when you go out, be prepared for all weathers!

Do you know the difference between a new moon, a full moon and a blue moon?

A **new moon** is a moon we cannot see from Earth! This is because the moon is so close to the sun at this point, that the side facing us is in darkness. In other words, the moon is between the Earth and the sun and therefore is not lit up.

A **full moon** is when the complete circle of the moon can be seen in the sky. The full moon in April is called the Pink Moon.

A **blue moon** happens when there are two full moons in the same month. The last blue moon was on 31 March 2018, and the next one will be 2 October 2020. This is because the moon goes through all of its phases in 28 days, whereas our months can be 28, 29, 30 or 31 days long. So every two or three years, there will be a month or two in the year when there are two full moons.

DID YOU KNOW...

In Roman times April was the month in which the goddess Venus was worshipped. She was the goddess of love, beauty and fertility.

CONSTELLATION OF THE MONTH

Hydra, the water snake, can be seen from January through to May, but it is at its highest point in the sky in April. It seems to suit the rainy month of April rather well to have a water snake as the constellation of the month!

The story behind Hydra comes from Greek myths. One day the sun god, Apollo, sent a crow to fetch him a cup of water. When the mischievous crow came back, he gave Apollo a cup with a water snake in it instead! Apollo was so angry that he threw the snake and the crow into the sky and they became constellations of stars.

There is another Greek myth that has a monster in it called Hydra. This was a monster with many heads which the brave and strong hero Heracles had to kill.

FESTIVAL FUN

1st April *April Fool's Day*

April Fool's Day is celebrated by people playing tricks on one another. Sometimes there are even April Fool's Day stories on the news. One of the most famous of these was in 1957 on the BBC television programme *Panorama*. The programme reported that in Italy there were spaghetti trees! Lots of people believed this because in 1957 not many people in Britain had eaten spaghetti, so they didn't know that it was made from flour and water and it definitely did not grow on trees . . .

Can you think of any good April Fool's Day tricks?

DID YOU KNOW . . .

There are a few unofficial rules about April Fool's Day tricks. The first is to do no harm – after all, the aim is to make someone look and feel silly. The second is that you can only play tricks before midday. If you try to trick someone in the afternoon, you become the fool!

FESTIVAL FUN

8th -16th April *Passover*

Jewish people celebrate Passover to remember how the Prophet Moses helped the Israelites escape from Egypt to a new life in the Promised Land. They left in such a hurry that the dough for their bread had not risen, so that is why Jewish people eat *matzo* at Passover today – a flat bread which is 'unleavened'. This means it has no yeast in it and so does not rise like a normal loaf of bread.

The Passover meal is called the *seder*. During the seder, Jewish families read and tell stories, eat special foods and sing songs, and children ask the adults questions about Passover.

12th April *Easter Sunday*

The Christian festival of Easter starts on the Thursday before Easter Sunday with a day called 'Maundy Thursday', when Christians believe that Jesus invited his followers to a meal called the 'Last Supper'. Easter ends on Easter Sunday, when Christians believe that Jesus came back from the dead. It is a time for new life and rebirth. Easter eggs are also popular on this day.

23rd April *Ramadan begins*

The month of Ramadan traditionally begins after the new moon, so the date changes from year to year. During Ramadan, Muslims hold a fast during the hours of daylight, which means they are not allowed to eat or drink from the moment the sun comes up until the moment it sets.

However, every evening, friends and family get together to have a lovely meal. People must also try not to gossip or fight during Ramadan. Muslims use the daylight hours to focus on saying prayers and giving money and possessions to charity. Some people try to learn the whole holy book, the Qu'ran, during this time!

EGG-CELLENT ACTIVITIES

Today, a lot of people in Britain give and receive Easter eggs over Easter weekend, whether or not they celebrate any religious festivals.

The Hunt is On!

Easter egg hunts are always exciting. You could ask an adult to hide mini chocolate eggs outside in the garden or in an area of your local park, or even while you are out on a walk. Then see how quickly you can find them – and don't eat too many on the way!

If the April showers are stopping you from going outside, why not have your Easter egg hunt in your home? There are plenty of places to hide eggs indoors. Make sure you find them all though – there's nothing worse than sitting on a forgotten Easter egg that someone has hidden under a cushion!

Decorating *Eggs*

You will need:

Hard-boiled eggs (cooled)
Wax crayons
White vinegar
Food colouring
Hot water
Different bowl for each colour dye
Tablespoon
Kitchen paper

1. *Draw a simple design on the egg with a wax crayon.*
2. *Make dye by mixing 1 tablespoon of vinegar with 1 tablespoon of food colouring in a small bowl and add ¾ cup of hot water.*
3. *Place a hard-boiled egg on a spoon and lower it gently into the bowl.*
4. *Leave the egg in the dye for a few minutes.*
5. *Lift out the egg and place it carefully on a piece of kitchen paper.*
6. *As the egg dries, the pattern you drew will appear through the dye!*

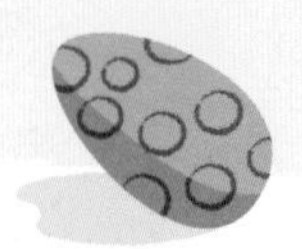

HOW DOES YOUR GARDEN GROW?

Once the weather warms up, April is a great time to start planting things. You don't need a big garden – in fact, you don't need a garden at all. A lot of flowers, fruits and vegetables can be planted in pots and grown on a windowsill or patio area.

Here are some easy plants to grow:

Geraniums

Lavender

Dahlia

Strawberries

Here are some plants you can grow from seed:

Runner beans

Sweet peas

Nasturtiums

Radishes

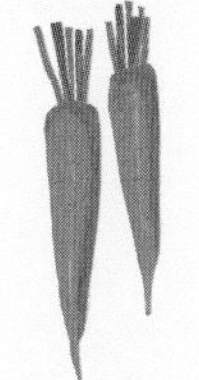
Carrots

Sunflowers

Watercress

TOP TIP

Don't forget to water your plants once a day.

EAT YOUR GREENS!

Most people do not like nettles because of the nasty sting you can get from the tiny hairs on the leaves. However, did you know that you can make the most delicious soup from them? Early April is the best time of year to make this recipe as the leaves are young and fresh and tender. It is fun to cook this outside on a campfire! If you do this, don't worry about using a blender – you can just stir the leaves in whole.

DID YOU KNOW...

The hairs on stinging nettles are full of formic acid, which is released when we touch them. 'Dead nettles' have no sting – they are recognised by their pretty white or purple flowers.

TOP TIP

To avoid a sting, wear gloves when you're picking nettles.

Recipe for *Nettle Soup*

You will need:

1 tablespoon of olive oil
1 onion, chopped
1 large potato, thinly sliced
1 l vegetable stock
400 g stinging nettles, washed
Salt and pepper
50 ml double cream
50 g butter, cubed
Crusty bread to serve

Large saucepan
Wooden spoon
Hand blender

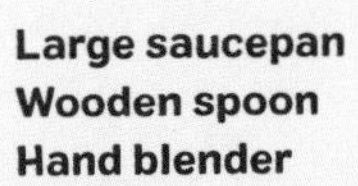

1. *Heat the oil in the saucepan over a medium heat.*
2. *Add the onion and potato and cook for 10 minutes until the vegetables have softened.*
3. *Add the stock and cook for 15 minutes.*
4. *Add the nettle leaves and cook on a lower heat for one minute.*
5. *Ask an adult to help you blend the soup.*
6. *Add some salt and pepper and pour in the cream.*
7. *Add the butter and stir in.*
8. *Serve with warm, crusty bread. Delicious and nutritious!*

PARK LIFE

There's lots going on in local parks now that the days are longer and lighter. Why not join a park run? You don't have to be a fast runner, so you can chat as you run if you like! And there's often a park café nearby where you can go afterwards to have a well-earned snack and drink.

Look at the website **www.parkrun.org.uk** to find out where your nearest junior park run is. You will need to ask an adult to help you register online before you join a park run.

If running is not for you, take a scooter, skateboard or bike to the park. Or ask an adult if you can volunteer to walk a dog from your local dogs' home if there is one near you. (Or walk your own dog, of course!)

Whatever you choose to do, getting outside and breathing in the spring air will make you smile.

BIRDS ON THE MOVE

The birds are getting noisier now! You might find that you are woken up earlier by the sound of a wood pigeon cooing loudly outside your window. Then other smaller birds join in with their different sounds. This is called the 'dawn chorus'. If you've got time in the morning, it's lovely to lie in bed and just listen to the music the birds make – it's like having a free concert right outside your window!

More and more birds are finding their way back to Britain after the winter. Look out for the first swallows, swifts and house martins later in the month.

The bird that people think of most in April is the cuckoo. It spends the winter in Africa but comes back to Britain during this month.

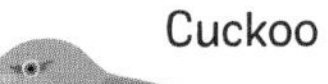

DID YOU KNOW...

★ It is traditional for people to write to *The Times* newspaper when they hear the first cuckoo of spring!
★ Each spring a female will lay between 12 and 22 eggs, all in other birds' nests.
★ A female cuckoo will lay her eggs in a nest belonging to the same kind of bird that looked after her when she was a chick.
★ Adult cuckoos move back to Africa as soon as their chicks are hatched. This can be as early as the end of June.
★ Young cuckoos follow their parents back to Africa several weeks later.

MAY

SPECIAL DAYS

1st Beltane (pagan celebration)/May Day

4th Early May bank holiday

21st Ascension Day (Christian celebration)

24th Eid al-Fitr (end of Ramadan)

25th Spring bank holiday

31st Whitsun/Pentecost (Christian celebration)

ANNIVERSARIES

75 years ago . . .

On 8 May 1945, the end of the Second World War was declared in Europe. More than one million people celebrated in the streets in Britain and the day became known as VE Day (Victory in Europe Day).

200 years ago . . .

On 12 May 1820, the nurse Florence Nightingale was born. She is sometimes called the 'Lady with the Lamp' and is best known for her care of sick and wounded soldiers during the Crimean War.

"Ne're cast a clout till May be out!"

This old country saying means that you should not rush to pack away your winter clothes until the month of May is over – or until the May flowers (also called 'hawthorn') are out in the hedgerows. This is because the weather can change quickly at this time of year. The air temperature is usually about 11°C–14°C, but in recent years it's become as hot as 25°C, as hot as a midsummer's day!

It is tempting on days like this to run about in shorts and a T-shirt. But be careful – you might go out in the morning dressed for summer only to feel chilly by lunchtime when the clouds roll in. So if a grown-up tells you to take a jumper with you to the park on a boiling hot May morning, it might not be as silly as it sounds!

Why is May Called May?

Nobody knows for sure, but it seems likely that this month was named after the Greek goddess Maia who was goddess of fertility. Her festival is still celebrated by some people on 15th May.

The Anglo-Saxons called this month *Thrimilci* (pronounced: 'three milky') because May was the month in which the cows were eating so much rich green grass that they could be milked three times a day.

May Birth Signs

Taurus The sign of the bull. Some people believe that anyone with a birthday which falls between 20th April and 21st May is born under this sign. They are supposed to be sensible and good at making and fixing things.

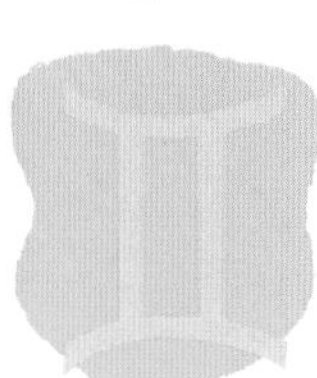

Gemini The sign of the twins. Anyone born between 21st May and 21st June is a Gemini. They are supposed to be very chatty!

The Sky at Night

This month there will be a full moon on 7th May. The full moon in May is known as the Flower Moon.

DID YOU KNOW...

No month of the year begins or ends on the same day as May.

Meteor Shower *Eta Aquariids*

These meteors usually fall sometime between 19th April and 28th May. This year, you should be able to see the shower from the night of 6th May to the morning of 7th May. About 30 meteors will fall each hour. The shower is formed by particles of dust left behind by Halley's Comet. This comet has been known about since ancient times and is the only comet that can be seen from Earth without using a telescope.

If you want to see the meteor shower, you will have to stay up late or get up very early! The best spot to see it from will be a very dark place from about midnight. The meteors can appear anywhere in the sky.

FESTIVAL FUN

1st May *Beltane*

The old Gaelic word *Beltane* means 'bright fire'. This ancient pagan festival celebrates the return of summer and is also known as 'The Feast of the Good Fires'. It marks the time of year halfway between the spring equinox and the summer solstice.

Long ago, it was a time when farmers let their cows and sheep back out into the fields after the cold weather. To make sure that their animals would stay healthy, the farmers would light big bonfires and burn special herbs on them. They would then make their animals walk in between the fires so that they could breathe in the purifying smells. This was supposed to protect them from illness.

1st May *May Day*

May Day celebrations are often mixed in with Beltane bonfires. A May queen is chosen and either two people carry her, or she rides through the streets on a cart pulled by a horse. The cart is covered in flowers and the May queen wears flowers in her hair. She sometimes has a man or boy with her representing the Green Man, who is the pagan god of nature. People dance around a maypole, which is a long stick with coloured ribbons coming from the top. Each person takes a ribbon and dances around the pole, weaving in and out of each other until the pole is tightly wrapped in the ribbons. This is done to symbolise how the growing strength of the sun is finding its way into the land. Traditionally, May Day was a time for weddings and lots of parties.

24th May *Eid al-Fitr*

Eid al-Fitr is an Islamic festival that is celebrated by Muslims all over the world. It is the day which ends Ramadan and it falls on or near the date of a new moon. During Eid, Muslim people celebrate with delicious food, by praying and by giving money to charity.

31st May *Pentecost or Whitsun*

Pentecost or Whitsun is the eighth Sunday after Easter. On this day, Christians remember that God sent the Holy Spirit to be with the followers of Jesus. In Britain the festival borrowed some ideas from the festival of Beltane, making it yet another celebration of summer arriving. In the north west of England some churches and chapels still hold 'Whit Walks' – parades that include brass bands, choirs and girls dressed in white.

GATHERING BUDS IN MAY

May is the month for wild flowers. It seems as though nature finds any excuse to sprinkle the roadsides, paths, woodlands and parks with colour. Even the most boring journeys are made more enjoyable by looking out of the window at the burst of colour.

Why not take your nature notebook with you and note down or draw what you see? If you have permission from the owner of the flowers, you can also pick one or two and press them when you get home – but be careful not to pick too many as bees and other insects need flowers for food.

How to *Press Flowers*

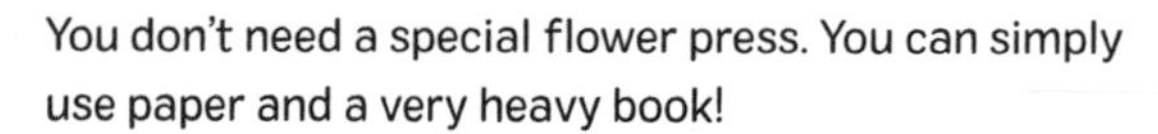

You don't need a special flower press. You can simply use paper and a very heavy book!

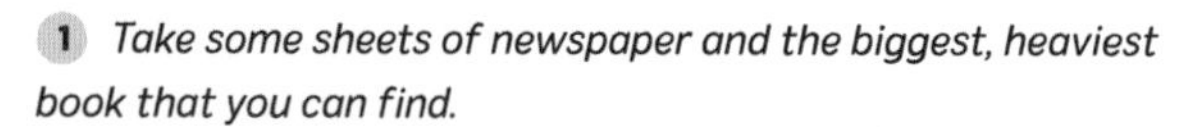

1. *Take some sheets of newspaper and the biggest, heaviest book that you can find.*
2. *Lay the flowers on the newspaper, opening them out as much as you can without breaking them.*
3. *Put another sheet of newspaper on top of the flowers.*
4. *Open the heavy book near the end.*
5. *Put the newspaper sheets into the book.*
6. *Close it and make sure the heaviest part of the book is on top of the flowers.*
7. *Leave for two or three weeks.*
8. *The flowers will have dried out and be pressed very flat. They will be very delicate so take extra care when lifting them off the newspaper.*

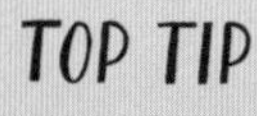

TOP TIP

Use your dried flowers to make bookmarks or even add them to homemade paper.

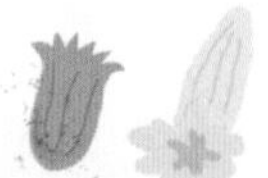
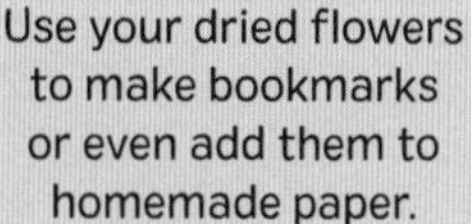

Make *Homemade Paper*

This takes a couple of days to make as you need to soak the recycled paper in water overnight. You can add some of your pressed flowers as decorations.

You will need:

Used paper
Washing-up bowl
Water
Old pair of tights
Old wooden picture frame or wire coat hanger bent into a square
Food processor
Shallow baking tray
Decorations such as flowers, leaves and seed heads
Food colouring or paint
2 small old towels
Rolling pin
Pegs

1. *Collect any old paper you can find.*
2. *Place it in a washing-up bowl full of cold water and leave it overnight.*
3. *While the paper is soaking, cut the tights so that you have one layer of fabric and then stretch this over the picture frame or coat hanger to make a screen.*
4. *The next day, ask an adult to help you fill the food processor half full with water.*
5. *Add a handful of wet paper and whizz it up until it looks like a thick milkshake.*
6. *Pour the mixture into a baking tray and add the flowers, leaves and seed heads. Add food colouring or paint if you want.*
7. *Place your screen face-down in the mixture and gently move it around to coat it with an even amount of pulp.*
8. *Lift the screen out and let it drain on a draining board or over the washing-up bowl.*
9. *Once a lot of the water has dripped out, put the paper on an old towel, place another towel on top and use the rolling pin to squeeze out any water that is left.*
10. *Hang the paper up using pegs on the washing line or somewhere warm and dry.*

TOP TIP

Ask a grown-up to help you with the food processor.

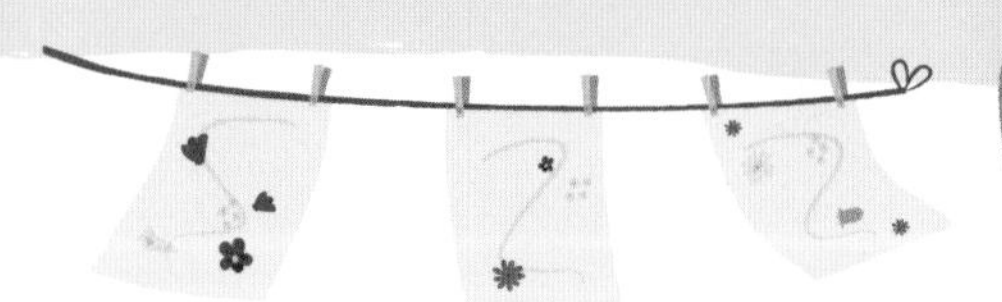

WILD-FLOWER SPOTTER'S GUIDE

See if you can spot any of these wild flowers in parks, on woodland walks or in the garden:

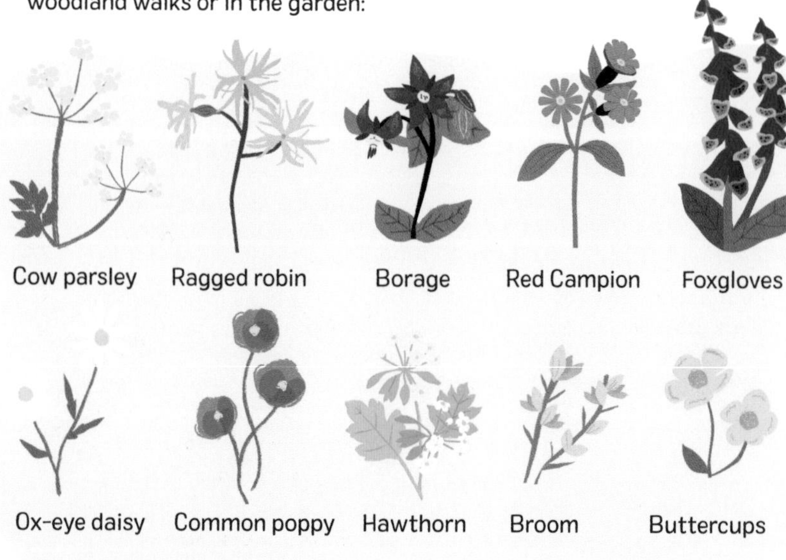

Down by the River

If you can get to a river in May, you will see the water looking at its most beautiful. There is so much to see, so take your nature notebook with you! Water lilies start to bloom during this month and they attract pretty insects such as banded demoiselle damselflies.

There are lots of families of mallard ducks around at this time of year – see how many tiny ducklings you can spot. Some families have up to twelve ducklings and they can be seen swimming in a line behind their mothers.

TAKE ME TO THE RIVER

Look out for beautiful waterside plants such as bulrushes and yellow irises. If you are very eagle-eyed you might spot a frog or fish jumping from the water!

You might also see a grey heron. They are large, serious-looking birds. Some people say they look like old professors!

How to Skim a Stone

'Skimming a stone' means throwing a stone over the surface of some water so that it bounces across the top without sinking straight away.

Once you have picked a stretch of calm water, you must find the perfect stone or pebble. The best 'skimmers' are flat and smooth.

Hold the stone loosely between your thumb and first finger. Tuck the other fingers underneath the stone to gently 'cup' it in your palm.

Hold your hand so that the front of the stone is pointing slightly upwards. Keep your elbow close to your body, then swing the stone from hip-height and whip your hand around.

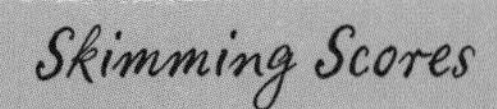

Ratings Table:

0 bounces: more practice needed!

1-2 bounces: well done

3-4 bounces: incredible

5-6 bounces: expert

7+ bounces: show-off!

The moment you let go, your first finger should be pointing in the direction you want your stone to go!

BABY WILD ANIMAL SPOTTING!

There are so many more animals around in May – many of them are babies. May is the perfect time for spotting young fox cubs or badgers. If you have ever watched *Springwatch* on the BBC, you will have seen how active these animals are, particularly at night.

A simple way to try spotting wildlife at night is to dress in dark clothing and sit very quietly in the garden while the sun goes down. Foxes, badgers, hedgehogs and bats become more active in the early evening. They come out of their homes looking for slugs, worms and insects to eat. Now that the weather is warmer, there is a lot more food around!

Hedgehogs

These lovely little animals are sadly becoming very rare. There are now fewer than half the number of hedgehogs in the wild since the year 2000. This is possibly because there are fewer hedges for them to live in as so many hedgerows have been replaced with fences. The other problem is traffic. Many hedgehogs are killed on the roads. Some towns have special 'Hedgehog Crossing' signs to warn drivers to go slowly and look out for the creatures.

If you would like to get a hedgehog sign to put up where you live, visit **www.britishhedgehogs.org.uk**

TOP TIP

Tinned cat food is a favourite treat for badgers, foxes and hedgehogs.

Bats

There are 18 different types of bat in the UK! They are a protected species because, like the hedgehog, their numbers are declining. Bats like to stay away from humans. However, sometimes they can be found living in attic spaces in buildings. If you find you have bats living in your home, do not worry. They will not chew wires or make nests. You should not try to pick them up, though, as this might frighten them and they may bite. Instead, you should ask an adult to contact the Bat Helpline to find out how to deal with the bats safely.

DID YOU KNOW...

Although we say 'as blind as a bat', this is not true – bats can see well, just not far.

Visit **www.bats.org.uk** to find out more.

Build a *Bug Hotel*

Insects and spiders are gardeners' friends! Encouraging small creatures such as bees, beetles and woodlice into your garden at home or school will help the plants to grow – so you'll be doing everyone a favour if you build a lovely shelter for the minibeasts outside.

You will need:

Bricks with holes in
Wood
Old logs
Straw
Moss
Dry leaves
Woodchips
Old terracotta plant pots
Old roof tiles
Bark
Pine cones
Sand
Soil
Hollow bamboo canes
Dead hollow stems from plants
Roofing felt

1. *Choose the spot where you want your hotel to be. Damp places are best for most bugs, but if you want to attract bees you'll need a sunnier spot.*
2. *Put some bricks on the ground to make a strong base, leaving some gaps between them – an H-shape is best.*
3. *Lay planks of wood across the bricks to make a 'floor'.*
4. *Cover the planks with dead wood and bark – beetles, centipedes and woodlice will love this. Spiders, too!*
5. *Put some more bricks or blocks of wood on the edges of the 'floor' to add another level.*
6. *Pack this next level with bamboo or other hollow stems for insects to crawl into.*
7. *Keep adding layers filled with other materials until you have the kind of hotel you want.*
8. *To add a roof, you can nail roofing felt on to the last area of wood – ask an adult to help.*

TOP TIP

Larger holes made from broken flowerpots or tiles are wonderful homes for toads and frogs.

JUNE

SPECIAL DAYS

13th The Queen's official birthday/ Trooping the Colour (the Queen's birthday parade)

20th Summer solstice

21st Father's Day

24th Midsummer's Day

29th Shavuot (Jewish 'festival of weeks')

ANNIVERSARIES

80 years ago . . .

On 18 June 1940, the British Prime Minister, Winston Churchill, gave his famous 'Finest Hour' speech. He gave it to encourage British soldiers to keep fighting for freedom in the Second World War.

150 years ago . . .

On 9 June 1870, the English author Charles Dickens died. He is well-known for many novels including *A Christmas Carol* and *Oliver Twist*.

"June damp and warm does the farmer no harm."

Summertime is here at last! It's time for strawberries and cream and barbecues. The roses are out in the gardens and parks, and of course there are lots of long, hot, sunny days to look forward to – right? Well . . . there will be some sunshine, but often we get excited and plan summer outdoor activities in Britain, only to find that the rain means we have to change our plans.

Nevertheless, this is the month to enjoy long days outside. When you get home from school it feels as though you have so much extra time to have fun! You can meet your friends in the park for football or just laze around chatting in the shade eating ice cream. June has the longest day of the year, so by 21st June you won't see the sun go down until around 10pm. This will change depending on where you live in the UK.

DID YOU KNOW . . .

The name for the full moon this month is a Strawberry Moon!

Average UK Day Length

	SUNRISE	SUNSET
1st June	04:54	21:50
21st June (Midsummer)	04:45	22:06
30th June	04:49	22:06

Why is June Called June?

The month of June was probably named after the Roman god Juno. She was the wife of Jupiter who was the king of the gods. Juno was the goddess of marriage. Some people think it is good luck to get married in June. The Anglo-Saxons called it *Sera Monath,* which means 'dry month'. (Maybe it didn't rain so much back then!)

Phases of the Moon in June 2020

Full Moon	Last Quarter	New Moon	First Quarter
5th June	13th June	21st June	28th June

Constellation of the Month

Cassiopeia was a vain queen in Greek mythology. The legend tells us that she was thrown into the sky as a constellation after enraging Poseidon, the god of the sea. She boasted to him that her daughter, Andromeda, was more beautiful than his sea nymphs. She should have known that it is never a good idea to make an ancient god angry!

FESTIVAL FUN

13th June *The Queen's Official Birthday*

This is always celebrated on the second Saturday in June. The Queen appears on the balcony of Buckingham Palace in London to watch the Trooping of the Colour. The soldiers wear special uniforms to show which regiment they belong to. Music is played by the Foot Guards' Band and the Band of the Household Cavalry, who are on horseback. There are 400 musicians in total!

The Queen gives awards called 'Birthday Honours' to people who have done something special in their lives, such as helping people in their community or charity work.

Birthstone and Birth Flower

You have a choice this month between the pearl and the moonstone. Both are supposed to bring health and long life. The official flower of June is the honeysuckle. Bees, butterflies and birds love this sweet-smelling plant.

29th June *Shavuot*

Shavuot is a Jewish festival during which Jews remember the day that God gave the Prophet Moses the holy scriptures, the Torah. Jews believe that Moses received the Torah from God on a mountain called Mount Sinai in Israel. Shavuot always comes 50 days after the second day of Passover. Women and girls light candles to welcome in the holiday, and some Jews stay up all night learning the Torah. All Jews go to the synagogue on the first day of Shavuot to hear the reading of the Ten Commandments. This is a list of laws for living a good life. They can be found in the Torah, the Qu'ran and in the Bible, too.

21ST JUNE SUMMER SOLSTICE

"*In winter I get up at night*
and dress by yellow candle-light.
In summer quite the other way
I have to go to bed by day."

ROBERT LOUIS STEVENSON (1850–1894)

It can be very annoying when you have to go to bed when the sun is still up! It is particularly hard to go to sleep on the longest day of the year. Pagans traditionally do not go to bed at all on this night! They stay up to welcome the sunrise and give thanks for its power and warmth.

One famous pagan summer solstice celebration happens at Stonehenge, a circle of standing stones in Salisbury in the west of England. People meet at the stones to watch the sunrise at about 4.45am. This is an act of worship and there is a lot of music and dancing.

The summer solstice is also known as *Litha*, which is an Anglo-Saxon word for 'midsummer'. Bonfires were lit on the tops of hills – some places in Britain still do this. The bonfire represents the strength, light and heat of the sun. Young men used to leap over them for luck!

Morris Dancing

Morris dancing is a form of English folk dance with music. The dancers wear bell pads on their legs to add to the music and they use sticks and handkerchiefs. The sticks are clashed together in a pretend sword fight. The handkerchiefs are used to make the dance flow as the dancers wave them in the air. They wear white clothing with colourful ribbons and sometimes brightly coloured jackets as well. Music is played on accordions, concertinas, violins, flutes, tambourines and drums. Dances have names such as 'Cuckoo's Nest', 'Bean Setting', 'Bonny Green' and 'Hunt the Squirrel'!

DID YOU KNOW...

The word 'solstice' comes from the Latin words *sol* (sun) and *sistere* (to stand still). People used to think that the sun was standing still in the sky at this time of year because it appears to stay in the same position all day.

STRAWBERRY FIELDS FOREVER

Who doesn't love fresh strawberries? They seem to burst on your tongue with the taste of summer sunshine. It is possible in some areas of the country to go to farms and 'pick your own', and that is the best way to get the freshest berries.

Strawberries grow very low to the ground in long rows. They are grown on straw to stop them rotting in the soil – which is, of course, how they got their name! To find your nearest 'pick your own' farm, go to **www.pickyourownfarms.org.uk**. You will be able to pick all kinds of fruit and vegetables yourself, not just strawberries.

Recipe for *Easy Strawberry Jam*

This is the most delicious jam – perfect for scones, sponge cakes or simply on fresh bread.

You will need:

Medium bowl
Wooden spoon
Large saucepan
Large metal spoon
Two saucers or small plates
Lemon squeezer
Teaspoon
Ladle
3-4 sterilised jam jars
Greaseproof paper, cut into circles
1 kg strawberries with leaves removed
750 g jam sugar
1 lemon
Coloured cloth
Elastic band
Ribbon

1. *Put the strawberries in the bowl and gently mix through the sugar with the wooden spoon.*
2. *Leave the bowl uncovered at room temperature for 12 hours or overnight.*
3. *The next day, put the two saucers in the freezer.*
4. *Tip the strawberry mixture into a large saucepan with the lemon juice and cook over a low heat.*
5. *Stir gently. When you can no longer see any grains of sugar, turn up the heat and bring the jam to the boil.*
6. *Boil for 5–10 minutes. To see if it has set, take the teaspoon and scoop a drop of jam on to one of the frozen saucers. If the jam goes wrinkly and doesn't run around the plate, it is ready. If not, keep boiling the jam in the pan and test it again in a couple of minutes.*
7. *Take the jam off the heat. Skim off any scum with a large metal spoon.*
8. *Leave the jam to settle in the pan for 15 minutes, then ladle into the jars.*
9. *Place a circle of greaseproof paper on top of each jar, then cover with the lid. You can decorate the lid with a circle of coloured cloth and hold it in place with an elastic band or ribbon.*

WARNING!

Always ask a grown-up to help you when you're handling hot pans and jars and make sure you wear oven gloves.

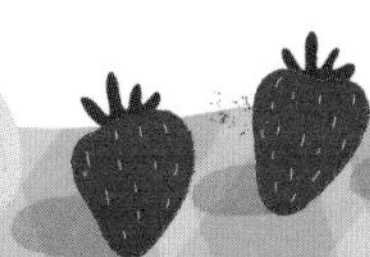

BUTTERFLIES AND CATERPILLARS

We're Going on a Caterpillar Hunt!

Caterpillars are among the most fascinating of small creatures. They eat so much and grow so fast! And then, before you know it, they have turned into beautiful butterflies.

You will need:

Jar or small pot
Cling film with holes in
Magnifying glass or minibeast pot

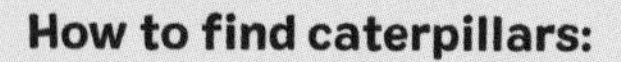

How to find caterpillars:

1. *Look for holes in leaves and missing parts of plants. Caterpillars spend every moment of every day munching their way through leaf after leaf. Sometimes the holes are as big as your fingernail, sometimes they are tiny pinpricks – it depends on the size of the caterpillar.*
2. *Can you find any little black blobs on the leaves? These are caterpillar poo. The proper name for them is 'frass'. If you see any, you'll know a caterpillar is nearby.*
3. *What about any tiny glassy green balls? These are butterfly or moth eggs, which means small caterpillars will soon be hatching.*
4. *Sometimes you might see strands of silk on a plant. It's not only spiders who spin silk, so do some caterpillars. They use them to make trails to walk around on or to make cocoons.*

When you find caterpillars, you can gently tip them into your pot to observe them. Don't forget to put some of the leaves you found them on into the pot so that your hungry caterpillars don't get even hungrier! Remember to return the caterpillars where you found them, so that they can turn into beautiful butterflies.

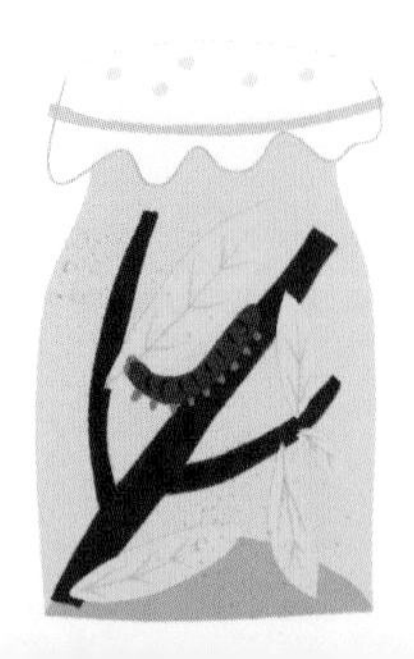

CAN YOU SPOT...
Large white (also called cabbage white)
Comma
Green-veined white
Male brimstone
Speckled wood
Holly blue
Orange-tip
Clouded yellow
Brown argus
Red admiral
Painted lady
Common blue

CARRY ON CAMPING

There is something very exciting about setting up camp in the summer, even if it's just in your own garden or in a park or field near your home. But it's not so exciting when the British summer lets us down by chucking rain on our tents!

If you are having a wet and miserable June this year, why not set up camp indoors? Ask an adult first, of course. In fact, you'll probably need an adult to help with this activity.

The best tent to use is a pop-up tent – the kind that you might take to the beach, for example – as these do not need tent pegs. If you don't have one of these, ask if you can use big cushions and blankets or a table and blankets to make your own 'tent' or den.

You can do this in any room where there is space. It's more fun if you don't do it in the room you normally sleep in, as that makes it feel more like camping!

Make a *Table-Tent*

If you are using a table, cover it with a cloth or blanket that is large enough to fall to the floor. Then, when you crawl in, you shouldn't be able to see anything outside the table-tent.

Fill the table-tent with soft cushions and some of your favourite games or toys, then get duvets or sleeping bags to snuggle up in.

If you have some colourful lights, such as Christmas lights, string them up around the entrance to the tent – they can be your 'starry sky'! Then you can switch off all other lights in the room and use torches to see by when you are inside the tent.

Campfire Food Indoors

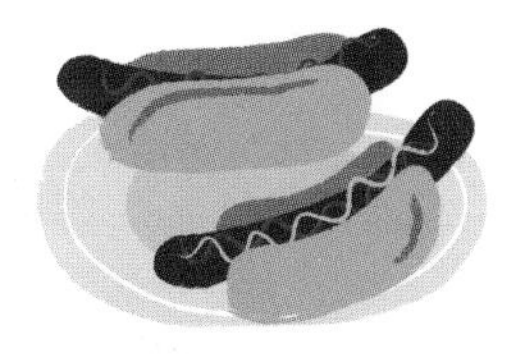

Ask if you can cook some sausages in the oven and make hotdogs to eat in your tent. For dessert you could try making 's'mores'. These are traditional American campfire treats made from marshmallows melted over the fire. The cooked marshmallow is then placed with a square of chocolate or a chocolate button between two crackers or biscuits. You can make them indoors by melting the marshmallows for a short time in the microwave in a bowl. Take them out carefully with a spoon and place them on a digestive biscuit with a piece of chocolate – they are just as yummy as the real thing!

DID YOU KNOW...

S'mores get their name from the fact that they are so delicious they make you cry out, "I want s'more!"

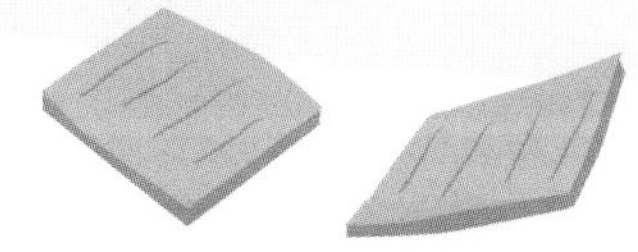

JULY

SPECIAL DAYS

12th Battle of the Boyne (Northern Ireland holiday)/Sea Sunday (Christian celebration)

15th St Swithun's Day

24th Olympics begins

25th St James's Day (Grotto Day)

31st Eid al-Adha (Muslim celebration)

ANNIVERSARIES

80 years ago . . .

On 10 July 1940, the Battle of Britain started. This was a battle fought in the skies over Britain during the Second World War between the British and German air forces. It lasted until 31st October.

80 years ago . . .

On 27 July 1940, the cartoon character Bugs Bunny first appeared in a cartoon called 'A Wild Hare'.

"Hot July brings cooling showers, apricots and gillyflowers."

SARA COLERIDGE (1802–1852)

It's the holidays! And this year the summer holidays are extra exciting as the Olympic Games will be held in Tokyo, Japan. So even if those irritating summer showers come along and stop you from going outdoors, you can watch some amazing athletes on the telly. Then, when the sun comes back out again, maybe you can have fun hosting your own mini Olympics in the park or garden.

Wherever you are this summer holidays, be sure to make the most of the long days with no lessons. The daylight is already fading now that the summer solstice is past, so it's important to enjoy the long summer days while they last!

Why is July Called July?

It was named to honour the Roman statesman Julius Caesar as it was the month in which he was born (12th July). Before that, it was known as *Quintilis* – Latin for 'fifth' – as this was the fifth month in the Roman year before the calendar was changed. The Anglo-Saxons called it *Heymonath* as this is haymaking time.

Phases of the Moon in July 2020

Full Moon	Last Quarter	New Moon	First Quarter
5th July	12th July	20th July	27th July

The full moon this month is known as the Buck Moon. Another name is the Thunder Moon because of the fact that there are often storms in the summer. Anglo-Saxons called it the Hay Moon because of haymaking or Wort Moon as it's the time to gather herbs (or *worts*) for using as spices and medicine.

DID YOU KNOW...

The Buck Moon gets its name from the new antlers that grow every summer from a buck (male) deer's forehead.

WHATEVER THE WEATHER

15th July *St Swithun's Day*

On St Swithun's Day there is a saying:

> "St Swithun's Day, if thou dost rain,
> for forty days it will remain.
> St Swithun's Day, if thou be fair,
> for forty days 'twill rain nae mair."

Thankfully, this is rarely true! St Swithun was the Bishop of Winchester. When he died in 862 CE, he was buried in front of the west door of the old Saxon cathedral building because he said he wanted to be buried outdoors. He lay there for over 100 years. When another bishop came along in 971 CE, he wanted to have a new patron saint, so he dug up poor old St Swithun on his feast day, 15th July, and moved him to a tomb inside! That day there was a terrible storm which lasted for 40 days and 40 nights. Many people believed that this happened because the saint was not happy about being moved indoors, so that is where the saying about the weather comes from.

25th July *St James's Day or Grotto Day*

There is an old tradition that on St James's Day, children would make 'grottoes' or little caves out of sea shells. This is because the scallop shell is supposed to be the symbol for St James who was one of the followers of Jesus.

Whitstable Oyster Festival begins on St James's Day. An old Kentish tradition says that Julius Caesar went to Britain because he loved the Whitstable oysters! The festival is a celebration of thanksgiving that still survives today.

Make a *Seashell Grotto*

If you go to the seaside this month, you'll be sure to collect some shells from the beach. Why not make your own St James's grotto by the sea? Make a sandcastle and then decorate it with as many different kinds of shells and pebbles as you can find.

SEASIDE COLLECTOR'S GUIDE

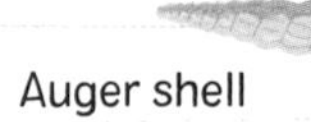

Auger shell

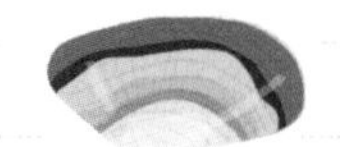

Banded wedge shell

Cockle

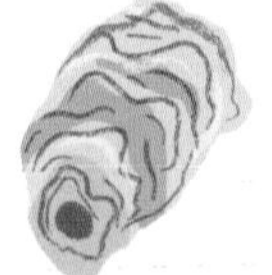

Oyster

Crab shell

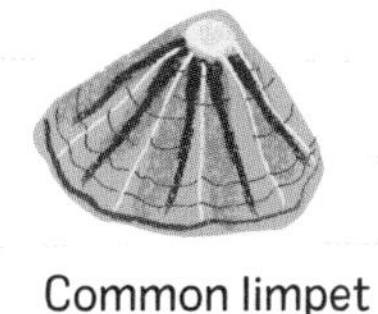

Common limpet

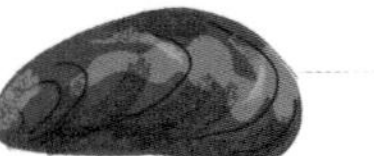

Common mussel

Dog whelk

Periwinkle

Razor shell

Shark's tooth

Slipper limpet

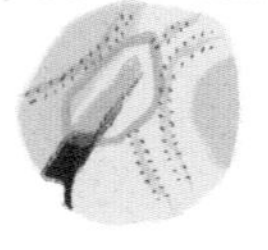

Sea potato

OLYMPICS

The Olympic Games are held every four years in a different city. This year, they will be taking place in Tokyo, the capital city of Japan, from 24th July to 9th August. Thousands of athletes will come together from around the world to compete in many different sports. The Summer and Winter Games take it in turn every two years. The next Winter Games are planned for 4th to 20th February 2022 and will be held in Beijing, in China.

DID YOU KNOW...

Legend has it that during the ancient Games, all fighting and wars were stopped until the Games were finished. Nowadays we know this is not true because the Greeks never stopped their wars! However, our modern Games have become a symbol for peace, as they bring different nations together in the name of sport.

Our modern Olympic Games were inspired by the ancient Games held in Olympia in Greece from the 8th century BCE to the 4th century CE. A Frenchman called Baron Pierre de Coubertin set up a committee which organised the first modern Games – they were held in Athens in 1896.

The ancient Olympic Games were not just sporting events. They were also religious festivals, held to celebrate the god Zeus. The athletes were all Greek and the main sports were running, jumping and throwing the javelin or discus. There were also wrestling and horse-and-chariot racing events.

No one really knows how the ancient Olympics started. One of the most popular myths is that Zeus and his son Heracles (known by the Romans as 'Hercules') were the creators of the Games. There is a legend that Heracles completed 12 very difficult 'labours' or tasks and then built the Olympic Stadium to hold the Games in honour of his father.

OLYMPIC FUN

Why not have your own Olympic Games? You can do this in the park if you don't have space at home. Choose some activities that all your friends will enjoy. You don't have to be able to run or jump to win a medal. You could set up a game like this:

Make an *Olympic Ring Game*

You will need:

5 paper plates
Red, green, yellow, blue and black paint
Some bottles from the recycling (washed)

1. *Make the rings by cutting the middle out of the paper plates.*
2. *Paint them the Olympic colours: red, green, yellow, blue and black.*
3. *Place the bottles on the ground, make a line about two metres from the bottles and ask your friends to stay behind the line. (You could use jumpers or jackets to make the line.)*
4. *Take it in turns to throw the rings over the bottles.*
5. *The one who 'hoops' the most bottles wins first prize.*

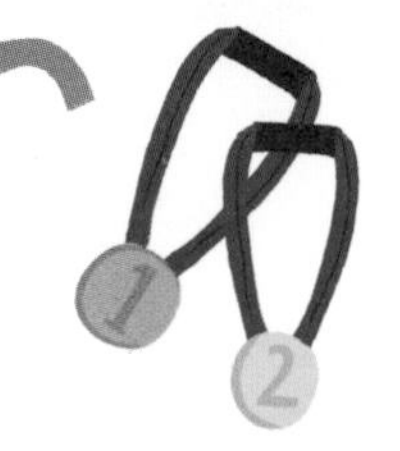

The Winner Takes It All

Make your own medals from salt dough so that you can give the winners a prize!

You will need:

Bowl
Sieve
Wooden spoon
Tablespoon
Skewer
Plate
Gold, silver and bronze acrylic paint
Ribbons

125 g plain flour
145 g table salt
120 ml tap water
1 teaspoon of vegetable oil

1. *Sieve the flour into the bowl.*
2. *Stir the flour while you add in the salt.*
3. *Add the water, one tablespoon at a time. Keep stirring the mixture until it looks like dough.*
4. *Add the oil to stop the dough from cracking.*
5. *Mould the dough into discs the size of the palm of your hand and about 1 or 2 cm thick.*
6. *Push the skewer through the top of the disc to make a small hole for the ribbon.*
7. *Place the discs on to a plate and microwave for 2 to 3 minutes or bake in the oven, at a very low temperature (100°C/210°F/Gas Mark 2) for about 2 hours, turning halfway through the baking time.*
8. *Wait until the discs have cooled before painting them gold, silver and bronze.*
9. *Allow the paint to dry and thread a ribbon through each hole.*

OUT IN THE GARDEN

There are lots of jobs to do now that the weather is warmer. The most important job you can help with is watering the plants if there hasn't been enough rain. It is always best to do the watering in the evening because if the day gets hot, the water can evaporate too quickly and the poor plants can get burnt. Tomato plants and runner beans need a lot of water at this time of year. So do any flowers you have growing in pots.

Another fun job you can help with is picking fruit – just don't eat too much as you pick! Lots of berries and currants will ripen this month: gooseberries, redcurrants, blackcurrants and raspberries.

When you've finished all your gardening jobs, find a lovely cool spot in the shade to rest. If you have two trees which are close enough together, you could ask an adult to help you put up a hammock. If you don't have a hammock, you could make a canopy instead by tying some string between two trees and hanging a sheet over it. Put a rug or some cushions under the sheet and you have a beautiful, cool canopy where you can read a book or have an afternoon snooze – or relax with a glass of homemade lemonade!

Recipe for *Homemade Lemonade*

There is nothing more thirst-quenching on a hot summer's day than a glass of homemade lemonade with lots of ice! Traditional lemonade is not fizzy like the kind you buy from the shops. It is made from a sugary lemon syrup topped up with tap water. You can of course use fizzy water if you prefer.

You will need:

Serrated knife
Food processor
Sieve
Large bowl
Wooden spoon

3 unwaxed lemons
140 g caster sugar
1 l of cold tap water (or fizzy water)
Ice or pre-frozen slices of lemon or lime

TOP TIP
Make your lemonade look on-trend by serving it in jam jars!

1. *Ask an adult to help you slice the lemons with the knife and throw the pips away.*
2. *Tip the sliced lemon and half the water into the food processor and blend until the lemon is finely chopped.*
3. *Hold a sieve over a large bowl and pour the mixture into the sieve.*
4. *Press the lemony mixture through the sieve with the wooden spoon to get as much juice as possible into the bowl.*
5. *Pour the rest of the water and the sugar into the bowl and give the mixture a stir.*
6. *Serve straight away in tall glasses with plenty of ice or add frozen slices of lemon or lime.*

CURIOUS CROP CIRCLES

July is the month when crop circles appear in some fields. They are best seen from high up. The circles are formed by the stems of crops being bent or trampled on. Sometimes the patterns made are incredibly detailed and complicated. They are often found near the ancient pagan standing stones at Stonehenge and Avebury.

Crop circles are formed overnight, and are usually spotted by farmers or passers-by the next morning. Some people believe that aliens come to Earth to make these patterns! But another theory is that they are actually made by human beings who go into the fields at night while no one is around. It is common to see crop circles appear after a night with a full moon.

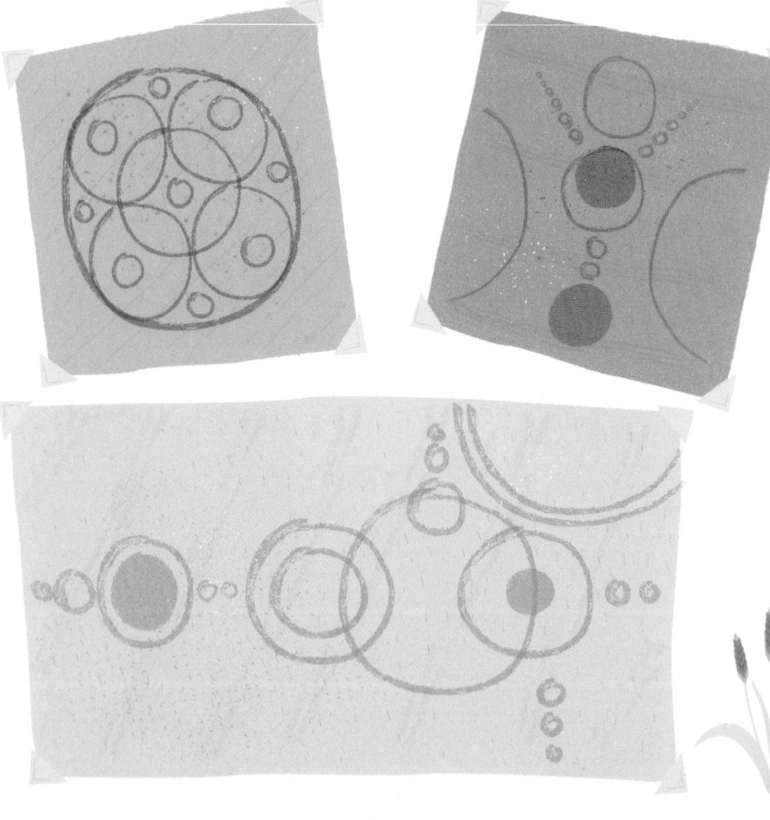

DOWN ON THE RIVER

Swan Upping

During the third week of July, the tradition of 'Swan Upping' takes place on the River Thames. This is a ceremony in which mute swans are caught by people in special boats called 'skiffs'. The swans are then 'ringed', which means they have numbered rings put on their legs so that we know how many swans there are. They are then released back to the river.

River Clean-Up

There are 'clean-ups' in rivers all over the UK. These are organised events in which people come together to help clear away plastic and other rubbish which sadly finds its way into rivers and streams and causes all kinds of problems for the wildlife that lives there.

Getting involved in a clean-up is a lot of fun if you get together with your friends and make a day of it. The events often happen in secret natural spaces which you might not have been to before. It also gives you a chance to help save the environment and make life better for wild animals. You can take the plastic you find to recycling centres or supermarkets which will take plastic bags and film wrap as well as bottles and cans.

If you want to find a clean-up near you, go to **www.ukrivers.net** and follow the links, or if you are near the Thames or any of the rivers and streams which flow into the Thames, look at **www.thames21.org.uk** for more information.

AUGUST

SPECIAL DAYS

1st Lammas/Lughnasadh (pagan celebrations)

3rd Summer bank holiday (Scotland)/ Raksha Bandhan (Hindu celebration)

20th Muharram (Islamic New Year)

22nd Ganesh Chaturthi (Hindu festival)

29th Notting Hill Carnival

31st Summer bank holiday (England, Northern Ireland and Wales)

ANNIVERSARIES

80 years ago . . .

On 30 August 1940, the British physicist Sir J. J. Thomson died. He is best known for winning the Nobel Prize in 1906 for discovering the electron. An electron is one of the tiny particles found in an atom, which is what we call the building blocks that make up the universe.

110 years ago . . .

On 26 August 1910, Mother Teresa was born in Skopje, the capital of Macedonia. She was a Catholic nun, best known for her work with the poor in India. After her death she was made a saint and is now known as Saint Teresa of Calcutta.

"Dry August and warm Doth harvest no harm."

In August, it can feel as though the summer holidays will stretch on forever. You can enjoy the long, sunny days and spend as much time outside as possible. Perhaps you will be lucky enough to go to another country for your holiday, but if not there is more than enough to do closer to home. Days by the seaside or down by the river or playing in the parks or woods near your home offer lots of opportunities for activities and fun things to do with your friends and family.

Or perhaps you are the sort of person who likes to do nothing at all on a hot, sunny day? Sometimes it's lovely just to find a spot of shade where you can read or snooze or sit and watch the world go by. Whatever you choose to do this August, make the most of all your free time and enjoy yourself!

Why is August Called August?

The Roman Emperor Augustus Caesar thought that since there was a month named after his great-uncle Julius, there should be one named after him, too! So *Sextilis* or the 'sixth month' was changed to August in the year 8 BCE in his honour.

The Anglo-Saxons called it *Weodmonath,* which means 'weed month' as so many weeds grow at this time of year.

Birth Flower and Birthstone

The flower for this month is the poppy, which represents strength, love, marriage and family. The stone is called peridot. It is an unusual olive-green colour and contains a lot of iron. Peridot is formed in the magma of volcanoes and comes to the surface when volcanoes erupt.

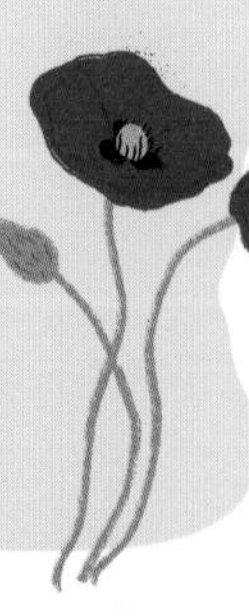

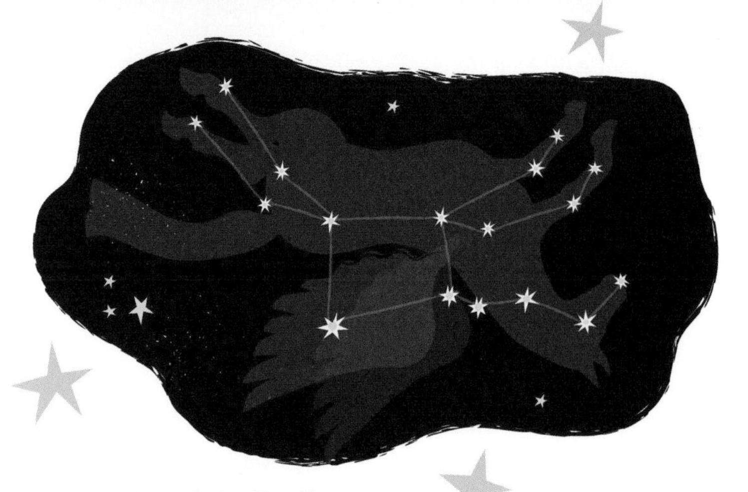

Constellation of the Month

You can see the constellation of Pegasus in the east in the early evening. It is a square of four very bright stars with trailing 'legs' and a 'head' coming off it. The brightest of the four main stars is called *Epsilon Pegasi* and is an orange supergiant. The star's name in Arabic is *Enif*, meaning 'nose', because it marks the place where Pegasus's nose is meant to be.

DID YOU KNOW...

The name for the full moon this month is the Sturgeon Moon. Sturgeon are an endangered species of fish. If anyone catches one, they must return it to the water. Sturgeon can be huge, growing to double the size of a tall adult person. Males can live up to 55 years, and females can reach 150!

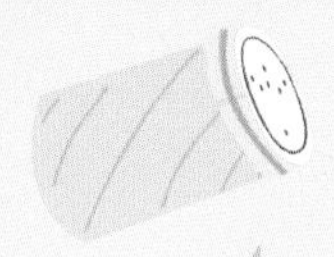

Make Your Own

CONSTELLATION VIEWER

If you can't get outside to look at the night sky, why not have a go at making your own constellation viewer? It is a good way of learning the different star patterns.

You will need:

Constellation circles (see page 109)
Scissors
Paper
Plastic cup
Pencil
Glue
Drawing pin
6 empty cardboard loo rolls, kitchen paper or wrapping paper tubes
Elastic bands
Sticky tape
Felt-tip pen
Chopping board (to lean on)

1. *Cut out each constellation circle using scissors.*
2. *Take a cup that is bigger than the constellation circle and draw around it to make circles on a piece of paper. Cut out the circles.*
3. *Glue a constellation on each large paper circle.*
4. *Cut lines from the outside of the large circle to the edge of the constellation circle.*
5. *Use the drawing pin to make a hole where each of the stars is.*
6. *Put the paper disc on to one end of your tube, and hold it in place with an elastic band.*
7. *Use sticky tape to stick the loose ends of the paper to the sides of the tube.*
8. *Write the constellation name on the tube using the felt-tip pen.*
9. *Look through the empty end of the tube, pointing the constellation end towards the light – you'll be seeing stars!*

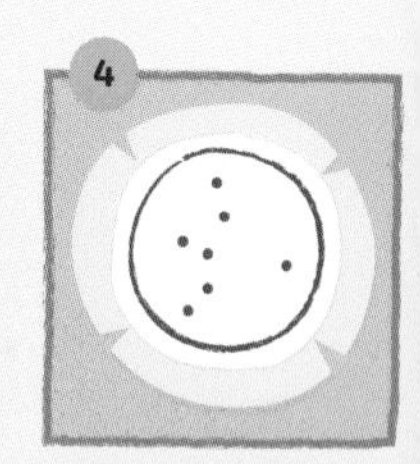

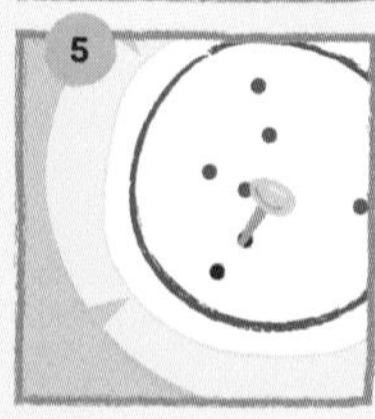

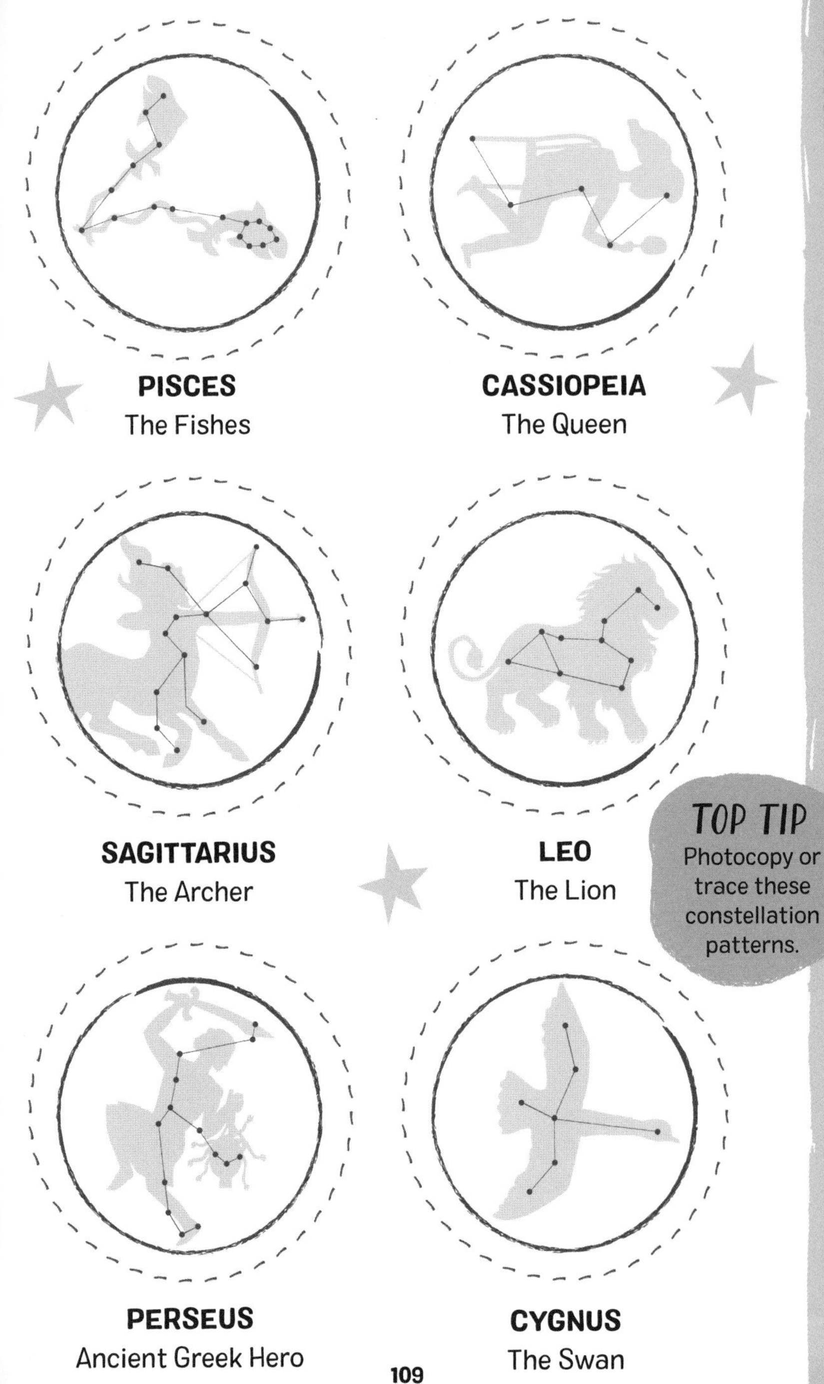

TOP TIP
Photocopy or trace these constellation patterns.

FESTIVAL FUN

1st August *Lammas*

Lammas is a pagan celebration of the first harvest, and is a time for giving thanks. The word *lammas* comes from the phrase 'loaf mass' which is a special celebration of the first grain to be cut in the harvest, and the first loaf to be made from that grain.

Lammas is also the name of the grain goddess, harvest queen and Earth mother. The harvest god is called John Barleycorn.

1st August *Lughnasadh*

On this day there is also an old Celtic festival called *Lughnasadh* – the festival of *Lugh* or *Lug*, the Celtic sun king and god of light. The celebrations include feasting, market fairs, games, bonfire celebrations and circle dancing. This is a time to remember that the power and energy of Lugh (the sun) is now slowing down and the darker days of winter are just around the corner.

3rd August *Raksha Bandhan*

This is a Hindu festival celebrated at the full moon. The name *Raksha Bandhan* means the 'bond of protection'. The festival celebrates the relationship between brothers and sisters. During the festival, sisters tie a *rakhi* (the holy thread) around their brothers' wrists. The brothers in return vow to look after their sisters, and give them a present.

The best time to tie rakhi on Raksha Bandhan is during *Aparahna*, which is late afternoon.

20th August *Muharram*

Muharram is the Islamic New Year. The Islamic calendar is based on phases of the moon, and is 354 days long. This means that the date of the start of Muharram changes every year. During the month of Muharram, many Muslims fast and pray.

22nd August *Ganesh Chaturthi*

Today is the day that Hindus start celebrating the birthday of Lord Ganesha, the god with the head of an elephant. Communities get together to worship, have parties and decorate their houses with models and pictures of Lord Ganesha. He is known as the god of new beginnings and is supposed to bring prosperity, good fortune and success.

Recipe for *Buttermilk Bread for Lammas*

You will need:

Large mixing bowl
Wooden spoon
Measuring jug
Baking sheet
Greaseproof paper
Knife
Metal skewer
Coloured ribbon for decoration: gold, orange or yellow

550 g strong white flour (plus extra for dusting)
1 teaspoon of bicarbonate of soda
Pinch of salt
Handful of seeds
500 ml buttermilk (or 250 ml whole milk mixed with 250 ml full fat Greek yoghurt)

1. *Heat the oven to 190°C/170°C fan/Gas Mark 5.*
2. *Place the flour, bicarbonate of soda, salt and seeds in the large bowl and mix well with your hands or the wooden spoon.*
3. *Make a dip in the centre with your fingers.*
4. *Pour in the buttermilk or yoghurt-and-milk mixture.*
5. *Mix well with the wooden spoon or your hands until the dough feels springy. If the dough is too sticky, just add a little more flour.*
6. *Turn the dough out on to a baking sheet lined with greaseproof paper and sprinkle with a fine dusting of flour. Then pat the dough with your hands until you have a round shape.*
7. *Take a knife and cut a cross into the top of your loaf so you have four sections, one for each season.*
8. *Place in the preheated oven for about 25–30 minutes. When the loaf is golden-brown, and a metal skewer stuck into the middle of the loaf comes out clean, the bread is probably ready.*
9. *Ask an adult to help you take the bread out and tap it on the underneath. If you hear a hollow sound, this means that the loaf is done.*
10. *Now tie a bright ribbon around the loaf and share it with your family and friends. Eat it fresh, as soon as it is made if you can.*

WARNING!
Ovens are hot, so ask an adult to help and wear oven gloves!

DID YOU KNOW...

Pagans give thanks before eating the Lammas loaf. They turn it three times saying:

"From the fields and through the Stones,
into fire, Lammas Bread.
As the wheel turns may all be fed.
Goddess Bless."

MORE FUN AND GAMES

The Olympic Games will not come to a complete stop in July! The Summer Paralympic Games will take place from 25th August to 6th September and are held for athletes with disabilities. The idea for the Paralympics came from a man called Dr Ludwig Guttmann. He had a hospital in Stoke Mandeville in Britain during the Second World War which looked after servicemen and women who had been badly injured.

On 29th July 1948, Dr Guttmann organised the first competition for wheelchair athletes which he called the 'Stoke Mandeville Games'. Sixteen people took part in the competition. In 1952, some Dutch people took part as well, so the name of the games was changed to the 'International Stoke Mandeville Games'.

In 1960, the Games became known as the Paralympic Games. They took place in Rome in Italy in 1960 and there were 400 athletes from 23 countries. In 1976, the first Winter Paralympic Games were held in Sweden.

ROCK POOLING

Who doesn't love the seaside on a hot summer's day? Even if you can't swim, perhaps you could find some rock pools to explore? The best time to do this is at low tide on a calm day when the sea has gone out and left water behind in the dips and hollows between the rocks. There's a lot to see in these miniature underwater worlds, so make sure you take your nature notebook with you – and try not to drop it in the water! Take a net and a bucket, too – that way you can take a closer look at some of the sea's minibeasts.

Remember to always be kind to the creatures you find and return them to their rock-pool homes after you have looked at them.

MAGICAL MOTHS

Some people find moths annoying, but they are extremely beautiful and it is worth observing them up close to see the intricate patterns on their wings. Use this spotter's guide to help you identify some:

CAN YOU SPOT...

Large yellow underwing

This moth has narrow, rounded top wings. They are either a reddish or blackish brown with a mottled pattern. The wings underneath are orange and have a black band along the edge.

Burnished brass

This moth is a gorgeous mix of orange, brown and gold, with panels of metallic greenish-yellow.

Setaceous Hebrew character

This is a very common moth. Look for the striking pale triangle which sits on either side of the wings.

Ruby tiger

This moth is bright red and has a cute furry head. Its 'woolly bear' caterpillars are a favourite food of the cuckoo.

Garden tiger

This moth has stunning spots and patterns on its wings. It squeaks at bats to let them know that it's poisonous!

Angle shades

This moth is often mistaken for a dead leaf!

Green carpet

This pretty moth has a green and black marbled pattern on its wings. As the moth gets older, the green fades to a yellowish or pinkish white.

Antler moth

This moth has a distinctive lightning-strike shape that branches off down either wing. You might even see this one during the day.

Recipe for *Blackberry and Apple Cake*

By the end of August some of the autumn fruits are already starting to ripen. Look out for delicious blackberries, bilberries and elderberries.

You will need:

225 g self-raising flour
1½ teaspoons of baking powder
225 g caster sugar
2 large eggs, beaten
150 g butter, melted (plus extra for greasing)
450 g cooking apples, peeled, cored and cut into chunky slices
200 g blackberries
Demerara sugar and cinnamon for dusting

Greaseproof paper
20 cm rectangular cake tin
Sieve
Food mixer
Wire rack

1. *Preheat the oven to 160°C/325°C fan/Gas Mark 3.*
2. *Grease and line the cake tin with the greaseproof paper.*
3. *Sieve the flour and baking powder into the food mixer and add the sugar.*
4. *Add the beaten eggs and melted butter to the food mixer.*
5. *Spoon half the mixture into the cake tin. Place the apple slices and blackberries on top.*
6. *Spoon the rest of the cake mix on top in blobs to cover the fruit as much as possible.*
7. *Bake in the oven for about 1½ hours, or until golden-brown on top.*
8. *Set aside to cool for 10 minutes, then remove from the tin and cool on the wire rack.*
9. *Sprinkle the cake with a mixture of demerara sugar and cinnamon.*
10. *Enjoy warm with ice cream as a dessert or cold with a cup of hot chocolate for a warming snack!*

SEPTEMBER

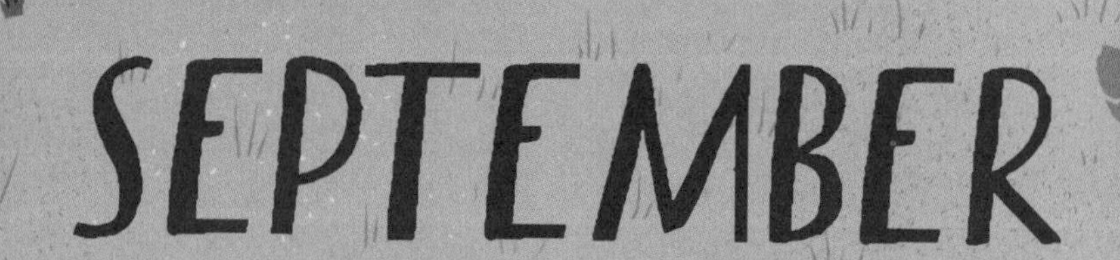

SPECIAL DAYS

19th Rosh Hashanah (Jewish New Year)

22nd Autumn equinox/Mabon/Harvest festival

28th Yom Kippur

29th Michaelmas Day (Christian celebration)

ANNIVERSARIES

50 years ago . . .

On 19 September 1970, the first ever Glastonbury Festival took place.

80 years ago . . .

On 7 September 1940, during the second World War, the Germans began bombing Britain in a campaign known as the Blitz.

400 years ago . . .

On 16 September 1620, the English ship the *Mayflower* began its voyage across the ocean, carrying people who wanted to start a new life in North America.

*"September days are here,
With summer's best of weather
and autumn's best of cheer."*

HELEN HUNT JACKSON (1830–1885)

September can be a golden month. Summer is fading, yes, but there is still warmth in the air, and the leaves on the trees are slowly turning from their different shades of green to the fiery colours of autumn. And, of course, the end of summer means the beginning of school again, which not everyone is happy about! But the days are still long enough to allow some time for fun in the park after school, so make the most of it before the clocks change and the countdown to winter begins.

Why is September Called September?

This month kept its original name from the Roman calendar. September comes from the Latin word *septem*, which means 'seven'. September was the seventh month in the year when the calendar began with March instead of January.

Constellation of the Month

Cygnus means 'swan' in Latin. The Romans took the word from the Greek *kyknos*. The ancient Greeks had many stories about swans. One of them was about the tragic hero Orpheus. He was killed and then transformed into a swan, after which he was placed in the sky. The constellation of Cygnus is quite easy to spot as it is shaped like a cross. It is in fact sometimes known as the Northern Cross.

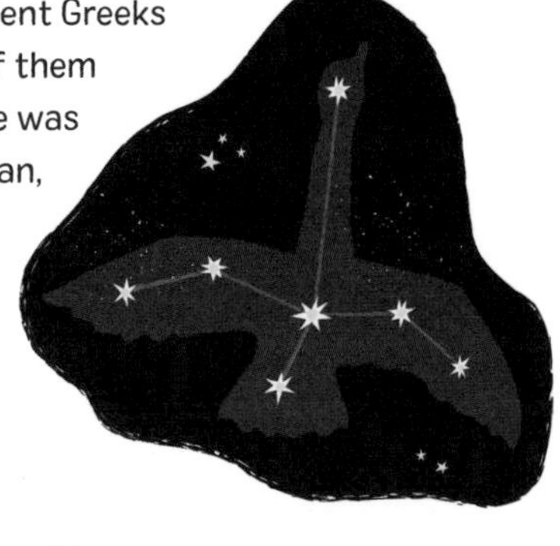

September Birth Signs

People born from 23rd August to 22nd September are said to be born under the sign of Virgo. They're supposed to be loyal, kind, hard-working and practical. They can also be worriers, are often shy and can end up working too hard if they don't make time to relax. They like animals, reading and nature and they don't like rude people! (Who does?)

People with birthdays on or between 23rd September to 22nd October are born under the sign of Libra. The sign is depicted by a set of weighing scales which represent a balanced personality. Librans are lovers of peace and harmony. Unfortunately, this means that they sometimes can't make up their minds as they can usually see both sides to every argument!

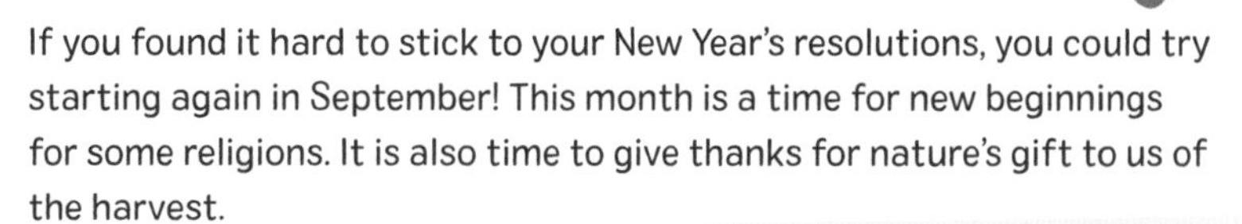

FESTIVAL FUN

If you found it hard to stick to your New Year's resolutions, you could try starting again in September! This month is a time for new beginnings for some religions. It is also time to give thanks for nature's gift to us of the harvest.

19th September *Rosh Hashanah*

This is a very important Jewish festival as it celebrates the start of the New Year in the Hebrew calendar. It is also a time for giving thanks for the birth of the universe and the day on which God created Adam and Eve. People light candles, enjoy special meals and come together to pray.

DID YOU KNOW...

Rosh Hashanah means 'Head of the Year'. Jews believe that the things we say and do during this time will control what happens for the rest of the year, just as our head controls our body.

22nd September

Mabon or Harvest Festival

The harvest festival is the closest thing we have to a day of thanksgiving in Britain. The word 'harvest' comes from the Old English word *hærfest* meaning 'autumn'. This was a very important time of year, as the success of the harvest could mean the difference between life or death for a whole community. In the past, even children had to help bring in the harvest. Then, as soon as it was over, everyone would return from the fields for the Harvest Supper. This was a huge feast with much singing and laughter.

28th September *Yom Kippur*

This is the holiest day of the year for Jewish people. It is a day for saying sorry for things you have done wrong and asking for forgiveness. Jews traditionally wear white and they fast and pray for up to 25 hours. They often spend most of the day in the synagogue.

29th September *Michaelmas Day*

The Christian celebration of Michaelmas, or the 'Feast of St Michael and the angels' falls near the equinox. Traditionally, Michaelmas Day was the time when new servants were hired or land was bought or sold, and money was paid back to people who had lent it. This is why most schools and universities start their new year around September; some of them even call the autumn term 'Michaelmas Term'.

BONKERS FOR CONKERS

'Conkers' is the name of a traditional game that is played using the seeds from the horse chestnut tree.

Prepare Your Conkers

1. *Choose two of the biggest, smoothest, roundest conkers you can find.*
2. *Ask an adult to make a hole through the centre of each one, either with a nail or a screwdriver, or even a drill.*
3. *Take two long pieces of string or garden twine – about 20 cm long – and thread a piece through the hole in each conker. Make sure you tie a knot in the bottom so that the conkers don't just slide off!*
4. *Find a friend and challenge them to a game . . .*

TOP TIP

When playing, hold the conker low, away from your face, and never flick or throw a conker near someone else's face.

How to Play

★ Stand opposite each other, holding the end of the string so that the conkers are hanging down.

★ Take it in turns to hit your conker against your opponent's.

★ The conker that breaks the other one gains a point.

WILD SEA, WILD ME

Believe it or not, September is the best month to go for a swim in the sea. This is because the water has been warming up over the summer and it is now as warm as it will be all year. If you do fancy a dip, take a grown-up with you and be careful to check the tides beforehand. Make sure you are swimming in a safe area where you can get in and out easily. Also take a good look at the waves first, as the sea can begin to get quite stormy and rough in September.

HARVEST TIME

September is harvest time which means there are lots of fruit and vegetables around to choose from. Sometimes, however, we find we have too many of one kind of fruit or vegetable and we don't know what to do with it! Especially if it is a vegetable that is not very popular . . .

Poor old courgettes are often seen as boring, watery vegetables, but they are actually delicious when fried, made into vegetable patties, or added to soups and sauces. They are also very good indeed in cakes! Try this recipe and you'll never see courgettes as boring again.

TOP TIP

You can ice the cake with a simple mixture of 100 g soft butter, 100 g cream cheese and 100 g sieved icing sugar. Yum!

Recipe for *Gorgeous Courgette Cake*

You will need:

Butter for greasing
2 large eggs
125 ml vegetable oil
85 g soft brown sugar
350 g grated courgette
1 teaspoon of vanilla extract
300 g plain flour
2 teaspoons of cinnamon
¼ teaspoon of nutmeg
½ teaspoon of bicarbonate of soda
½ teaspoon of baking powder
Pinch of salt
85 g chopped walnuts (optional)
140 g sultanas

900 g loaf tin
Greaseproof paper
Cheese grater
Sieve
Whisk
Two mixing bowls
Wooden spoon
Metal skewer

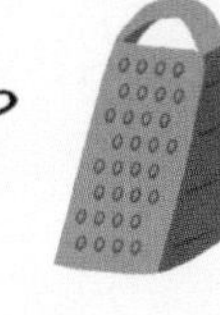

1. *Heat the oven to 180°C/160°C fan/Gas Mark 4.*
2. *Grease and line the loaf tin with the greaseproof paper.*
3. *Grate the courgettes and check the weight.*
4. *Leave the courgettes to drain in the sieve while you prepare the other ingredients.*
5. *In one bowl, whisk together the eggs, oil and sugar.*
6. *Add the courgettes and the vanilla extract.*
7. *In the other bowl, mix the dry ingredients.*
8. *Stir the dry ingredients into the wet mixture, then pour into the loaf tin.*
9. *Bake for about 1 hour or until a metal skewer comes out clean.*
10. *Leave to cool.*
11. *Enjoy warm with ice cream (salted caramel flavour is good with this!) or cold as a cake for afternoon tea.*

TOP TIP

Add some lemon or orange zest for a slightly different flavour or try using chocolate chips instead of sultanas and walnuts.

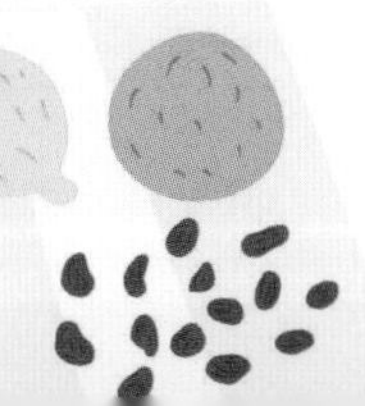

BE A NATURE DETECTIVE

Walk carefully through the woods, keeping your eyes open for any signs of where an animal has been. You might notice some leaves have been disturbed, or there is a hole under a fence where a creature has pushed its way through.

Look for a good track that shows you a lot of detail. You might need to gently push any leaves or sticks aside.

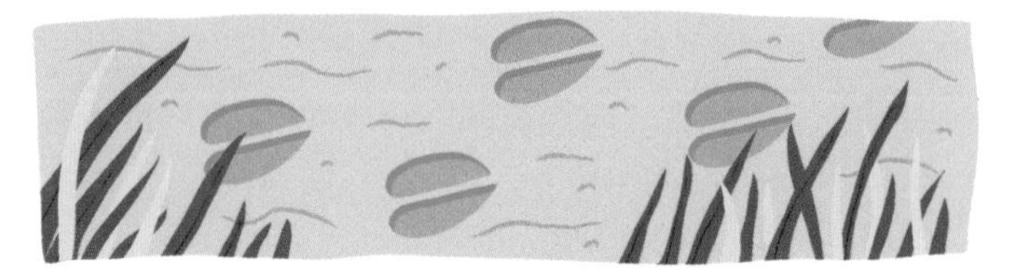

You could take photos of any footprints that you find, but why not make drawings of them, too? Drawing makes us concentrate harder on what we are seeing because we have to look closely to copy the details of the print. Just like a wildlife expert, you will learn and remember what the track looks like if you ever see it again.

You can then take your drawings home and compare them with the animal print guide on the opposite page. Can you identify the animals from their prints? Be sure to also make a note of the plants and the kind of landscape where you found the track. You can use your nature notebook for this. This will help you remember where you found the marks and to identify the animal, too.

Phases of the Moon **in September 2020**

Full Moon	Last Quarter	New Moon	First Quarter
2nd September	10th September	17th September	24th September

Harvest Moon

The full moon in September is known as the Corn Moon or Harvest Moon, depending on when it appears in the month. It is called the Harvest Moon before the 23rd September, or the Corn Moon after.

CREEPY CRAWLIES

Poor old spiders have got quite a bad name for themselves – so many people are scared of them! We shouldn't be frightened of them in Britain, though, as they are not dangerous and in fact they are very useful and do a lot of good.

Six Spidery Facts

★ People think there are more spiders around in the autumn, but actually it's just that we're more likely to see them at this time of year. This is because they are now fully grown and also because it's the mating season, so the males can be seen hurrying around trying to find a female.

★ House spiders don't particularly like baths – and they definitely don't like getting wet. It's just that they sometimes fall in and then can't climb out! This is especially true of large spiders which, unlike some smaller ones, can't walk up smooth surfaces.

TOP TIP

Try leaving strips of loo paper hanging into the bath to help trapped spiders climb out!

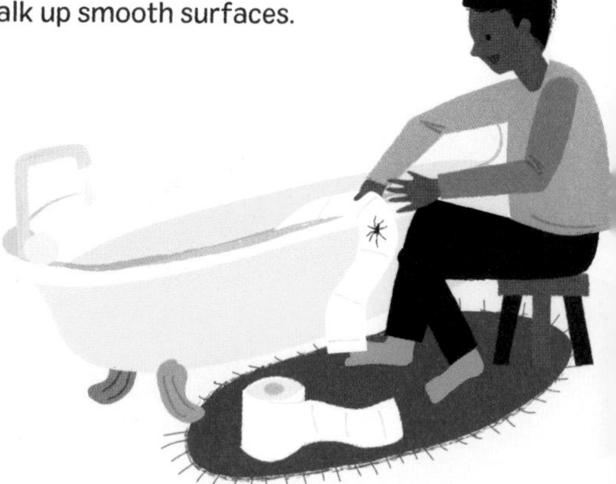

★ All British spiders use poison to digest their prey. However, they are not harmful to humans.

★ We live alongside so many spiders that we are never more than a metre away from one! Most are very small, so you probably won't even see them.

★ Very few spiders enjoy living in modern centrally-heated homes. Most of them would prefer us to take them back outside as they really like living in garages or sheds where they can hide in peace and quiet.

★ You might not like having spiders around, but they are useful because they eat other bugs that we also dislike. They are particularly keen on midges and mosquitoes. So remember – it would be a lot worse if there weren't any spiders around.

DID YOU KNOW...

The word 'cobweb' comes from the Old English word coppe, *which means 'spider',* and web, *which means 'woven fabric'.*

CAN YOU SPOT...

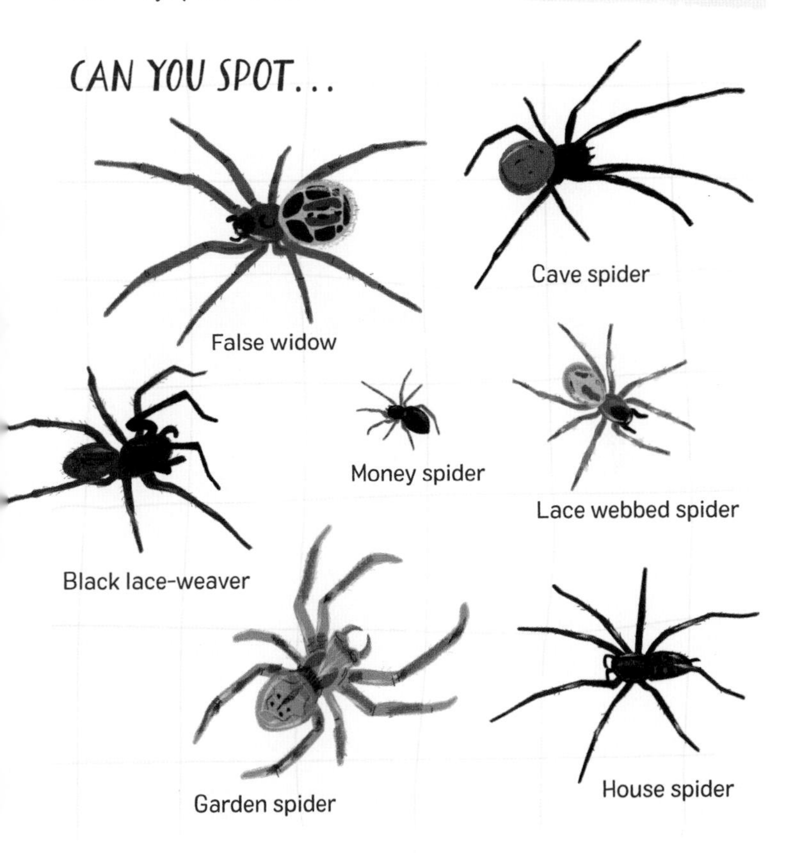

OCTOBER

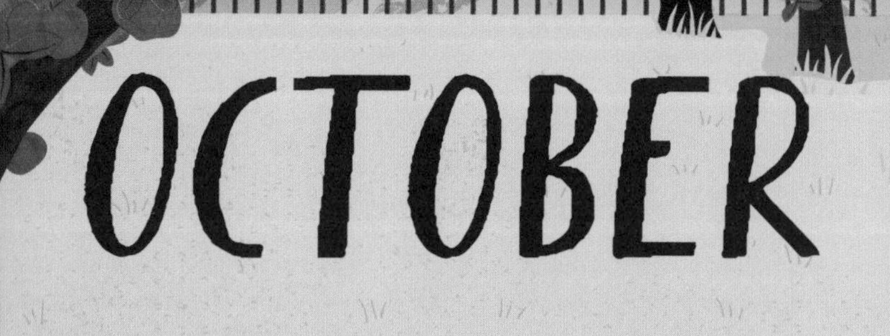

SPECIAL DAYS

21st	Apple Day
25th	October Daylight Saving
29th	Prophet's Birthday
31st	Samhain Eve (pagan festival)/All Saints' Eve (Christian festival)/Halloween

ANNIVERSARIES

80 years ago . . .

On 9 October 1940, the singer and songwriter John Lennon was born in Liverpool. He was famous for being one of The Beatles, a pop group who have sold over 600 million albums worldwide.

95 years ago . . .

On 2 October 1925, the Scottish engineer and inventor John Logie Baird sent the first ever television picture.

"Corn and grain, corn and grain.
All that falls shall rise again."

WICCAN HARVEST CHANT

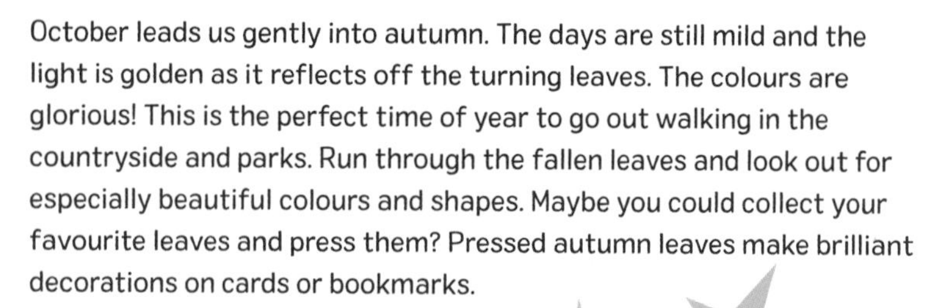

October leads us gently into autumn. The days are still mild and the light is golden as it reflects off the turning leaves. The colours are glorious! This is the perfect time of year to go out walking in the countryside and parks. Run through the fallen leaves and look out for especially beautiful colours and shapes. Maybe you could collect your favourite leaves and press them? Pressed autumn leaves make brilliant decorations on cards or bookmarks.

DID YOU KNOW...

When the Romans came to Britain they took the Celtic festival of *Samhain* in October and combined it with two of their own festivals: *Pomola*, which was a harvest festival, and *Feralia*, which was a festival for remembering the dead.

Why is October Called October?

October gets its name from the Latin word *octo* which means 'eight', and was named by the Romans during a time when the calendar year began with March instead of with January as it does now.

The Anglo-Saxon name for this month was *Winterfylleth* which comes from the words for winter and the full moon.

The Moon's a Balloon!

The October full moon this year is called the Hunter's Moon. It is also known as the Blood Moon because it can often be a striking red or orange colour. Of course, the colour of the actual moon hasn't changed! The moon hangs lower in the sky at this time of year, closer to the horizon, and so we are seeing it through more of the Earth's atmosphere. The gases around the Earth and the tiny particles in the air affect the way in which we see light. Orange and red light has longer wavelengths and so these are the colours we see reflected off the moon when it is closer to us.

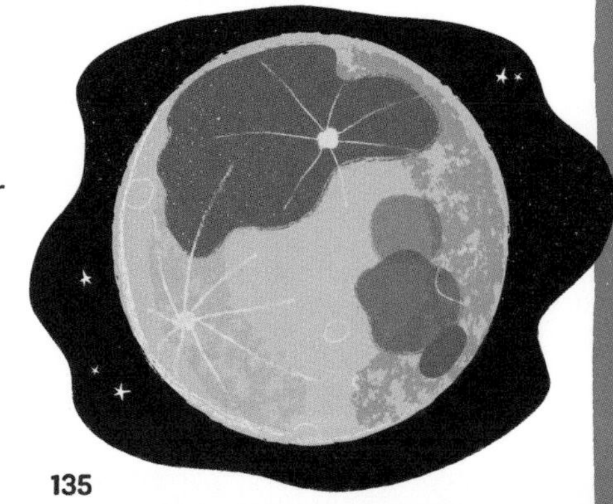

29th October *Prophet's Birthday*

In the UK and all over the world, some Muslims see this as a day to celebrate. In some countries there are street parades, the mosques are decorated and children read out poems about the Prophet's life. People can spend the day donating food and money to charity, too. Other Muslims see this day as a time for concentrating on the holy book, the Qur'an.

31st October *Samhain Eve*

The festival of Samhain (pronounced 'Saah-win' or 'saah-ween') comes from ancient pagan Celtic and Gaelic harvest traditions. Its name means 'summer's end'. It is a time for giving thanks for the end of the harvest and it marks the beginning of the coldest half of the year. Pagans celebrate by holding a feast and by remembering those loved ones who have died and are no longer with us. Sometimes people set a place at the table for these loved ones and put food in front of it as an offering to those who have passed on.

31st October *All Saints' Eve*

This is a Christian festival also known as All Hallows' Eve, Hallowed Evening or Holy Evening, which is how we get the name Halloween! On the evening of 31st October, some Christians begin three days of ceremonies and services to remember loved ones who have died and the saints ('hallowed' or holy people). It is traditional to light candles for those who have died and to spend time praying and remembering them.

31st October *Halloween*

Nowadays we associate Halloween with fun and games and dressing-up. But in fact, as far back as the 16th century, people had parties on 31st October, playing games and practising rituals to try and tell the future, especially about deaths or marriages in the family. This is where the game of apple-bobbing comes from. It used to be thought that the first person to bite into an apple would be the first person to get married!

Before pumpkins were brought over from America, people would use turnips or other root vegetables to make lanterns. These were carved with ugly faces in the hope that they would scare away evil spirits.

PUMPKIN CARVING

How about carving your own lantern? These look great as table decorations for a Halloween party or you can leave them outside your house to welcome trick-or-treaters.

You will need:

Medium-sized pumpkin
Large metal spoon
Chopping board
Medium bowl
Biro or marker pen
Sharp knife
Tealight
Wooden toothpicks
Scary Halloween vampire teeth

1. *Ask an adult to help you cut a small 'lid' off the top of your pumpkin.*
2. *Use the metal spoon to remove the seeds and scoop out as much of the flesh as you can.*
3. *Put the seeds and flesh in a bowl and put aside.*
4. *Draw a face on your pumpkin.*
5. *Ask an adult to help you cut out the eyes, nose and mouth.*
6. *Ask an adult to help you light a tealight and put it in your pumpkin.*
7. *Turn out all the lights! Your super scary pumpkin lantern is spookily ready for Halloween!*

TOP TIP

Use the flesh you have scooped out to make pumpkin muffins or pumpkin soup. You can also roast the seeds for a tasty snack!

Scary Faces

If you don't want to spend time cutting out lots of teeth for your lantern, here are three easier ways to give your pumpkin a spooky face.

1. Cut a large crescent for a mouth and then stick wooden toothpicks into the top and bottom lips to make lots of spiky teeth!

2. Make it look as though your pumpkin has been sick by filling the mouth with pumpkin seeds and letting them spill out of the mouth on to a plate.

3. Get some joke-shop vampire teeth and stick them inside your pumpkin's mouth – if you can get glow-in-the-dark ones, even better!

DID YOU KNOW...

In the early 16th century, a French explorer called Jacques Cartier came across pumpkins for the first time in North America. He said he had found *gros melons*, which means 'large melons'. The English heard this as pompions. The word has changed over time into 'pumpkin' which we use today.

APPLES GALORE

October is apple month! If you live in an area where there are a lot of apple trees, you might find lots of apples falling into the street. These are known as 'windfalls'. They might look battered and bruised, but windfalls are excellent apples to put in pies, crumbles and cakes. They make delicious apple sauce as well, which is yummy as a dessert with ice cream or yoghurt and also goes very well with roast pork. Always check windfalls carefully as there are a lot of sleepy wasps around at this time of year and they can sometimes be found slowly munching their way through apples that have fallen to the ground. You will also need to wash windfalls and cut out any bruised flesh before you use them for cooking.

Recipe for *Baked Apples*

If you can get hold of some lovely big cooking apples, this recipe is a wonderfully warming dessert for when the evenings get darker and colder.

You will need:

Chopping board
Sharp knife
Apple corer
Small bowl
Wooden spoon
Shallow baking dish

6 large cooking apples
50 g sultanas
2 tablespoons of light brown soft sugar
1 teaspoon of cinnamon
25 g butter
2 tablespoons of demerara sugar

1. *Preheat the oven to 200°C/180°C fan/Gas Mark 6.*
2. *Put the apples on the chopping board and ask an adult to help make a shallow cut in a ring around the middle of each apple.*
3. *Ask an adult to help you remove the core of each apple.*
4. *Mix the sultanas, light brown soft sugar and cinnamon with the wooden spoon in the small bowl.*
5. *Put the apples side by side in the baking dish with the holes facing upwards.*
6. *Gently push the sultana mixture into the holes, filling them up to the top.*
7. *Add a blob of butter to the top of each apple and sprinkle with demerara sugar.*
8. *Cook the apples for about 20 minutes.*
9. *The apples will go soft and gooey and the fruit will caramelise in the sugar. Serve hot with ice cream, cream or yoghurt.*

THE MIGRATION OF BEWICK'S SWANS

Bewick's swans spend April–September in an area of northern Russia called the Russian tundra, where they breed. Then, in October, to escape the fierce cold weather in the north, they begin a long journey, migrating south-west. Many of them find their way to Britain and stay here until March when they begin their journey back to Russia. They arrive in their greatest numbers in the east of England, but can also be seen in the Severn Estuary near Bristol in the west and also in Lancashire and Ireland.

DID YOU KNOW...

Sadly, there are fewer Bewick's swans than there used to be. In 1995, it was thought that about 29,000 of the birds came to Europe. In recent years, the number has dropped to around 18,000 and the numbers are believed to still be going down.

Top Four Facts About Bewick's Swans

1. These amazing birds can live for 30 years.
2. They tend to stay with one partner until one of them dies. Some have stayed together for up to 21 years.
3. Bewick's swans often return to the same wetland area every year.
4. The babies, called cygnets, stay with their parents for the whole of their first winter and their parents guide them on their first migration so that they know where to go.

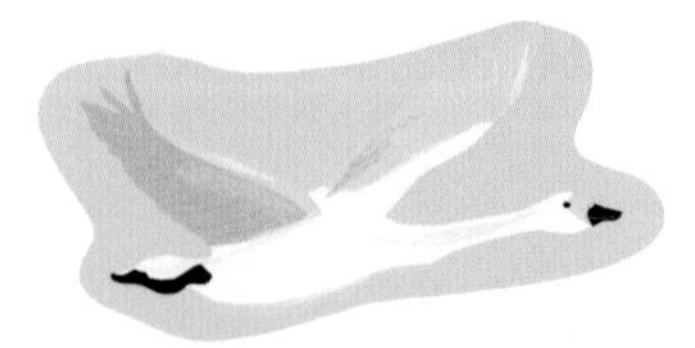

Know Your Swans!

There are three different swans to spot in Britain. Here's how to tell them apart:

Mute swan

The mute swan has a wedge-shaped head, a long S-shaped neck and an orange bill with a black patch at the bottom of it.

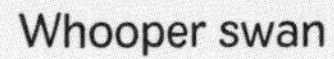

Whooper swan

The whooper swan has a long, thin neck which it normally holds up straight. It has a black bill with a large triangle of yellow on it. You will normally see whooper swans from September through to April, although some do stay in the UK all year round.

Bewick's swan

Bewick's swans have rounder heads than whooper swans. They have a smaller bill which is mainly black with a smaller patch of yellow on the side. They also have a shorter neck than the other types of swan.

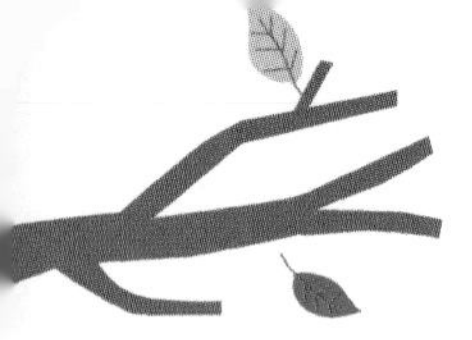

TIME FOR BED

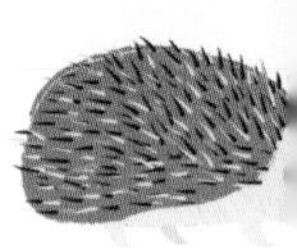

As well as birds and animals migrating, autumn is a time for some of them to hibernate, which means they go to sleep for the whole winter. There are not many creatures that do this in Britain, as our winters are not as cold as in other parts of the world.

Why Do Animals Hibernate?

It's not just because they like being warm and cosy – or lazy! Animals who hibernate aren't simply going to sleep – their bodies have adapted to make sure that they survive during the winter months. When they go into hibernation, their bodies slow right down so that they breathe more slowly, their hearts beat much more slowly and the temperature of their bodies drops. This means that they don't need to eat so much because their bodies are not using as much energy as when they are awake and running around. However, before they hibernate they make sure they eat lots and lots to fatten up so that they have plenty of energy in reserve during their long sleep.

THE DARK IS RISING

The days are getting shorter and shorter. However, we still have light evenings until the clocks change on Sunday 25th October. This means we get an extra hour in bed the night before. It can be confusing if you are a baby or a pet as it messes around with your mealtimes!

Why Do the Clocks Change?

We didn't always bother with changing the clocks. In the old days, people went to bed when the sun went down and got up again when it rose. Midday was several minutes earlier in the east of the country than it was in the south, and several minutes later in the west. This meant that town clocks across the British Isles showed different times. The building of the railway network changed all that because the time had to be the same all over the country, or people would not have had the faintest idea when to catch a train.

Then a man called William Willett suggested to parliament that if the clocks changed, we would all enjoy more daylight in the autumn and winter months. So, since 1916, the clocks have gone back one hour in October and in March the clocks have been put forward by one hour. This is known as 'Daylight Saving'.

TOP TIP

In spring, the clocks spring forward an hour, and in the autumn, they fall back.

NOVEMBER

SPECIAL DAYS

1st All Saints' Day (Christian celebration)
2nd All Souls' Day (Christian celebration)
5th Guy Fawkes Night (Bonfire Night)
8th Remembrance Sunday
11th Armistice Day (Remembrance Day)/Martinmas
14th Diwali (Hindu New Year)
22nd Stir-up Sunday (last Sunday before Advent)
29th First Sunday of Advent
30th St Andrew's Day (Scotland)

ANNIVERSARIES

85 years ago . . .

On 5 November 1935, a company called Parker Brothers launched the first game of Monopoly.

500 years ago . . .

On 28 November 1520, a Portuguese explorer called Ferdinand Magellan led the first European ships from the Atlantic Ocean across to the Pacific Ocean as part of a plan to sail around the world.

"So dull and dark are the November days.
The lazy mist high up the evening curled,
And now the morn quite hides in smoke and haze."

JOHN CLARE (1793–1864)

We can no longer deny it – winter is on its way! The shortest day is less than two months away, so it is no wonder that so many festivals this month celebrate light. Many festivals also focus on sweet-tasting food – a sweet treat can be just what you need when you've been outside, battling the cold! This is the time of year to tidy away the garden for winter, and a bonfire is a great way to get rid of dead leaves and wood.

Why is November Called November?

The word November comes from the Latin word for the number nine, *novem*. This is because, just like September and October before it, November keeps its name from a time when the calendar had only ten months.

The Anglo-Saxons called this month *Blotmonath*, which means 'blood month'. This is because it was traditional at this time of year to kill farm animals and preserve the meat for the winter months ahead.

Constellation of the Month

Taurus is the Latin word for 'bull'. Look out for this constellation in the east, where it starts the night low in the sky. If you look for the bright orange giant star called Aldebaran, that will help you find the rest of the constellation.

November Birth Signs

People born under the sign of Scorpio (the scorpion) on or between 23rd October and 21st November are said to be brave, passionate, stubborn and a true friend. They like the truth, facts and being right! They also like to have deep, long-lasting friendships.

Sagittarius is represented by a centaur – a mythological creature who is half-man, half-horse. People born under the sign of Sagittarius, on or between 22nd November and 21st December, are supposed to be generous and have a great sense of humour. They can also be very impatient and will often speak first and think after!

DID YOU KNOW...

The full moon this month is sometimes known as the Beaver Moon. The name comes from Northern Native American culture and was chosen because beavers build their dams at this time of the year to get ready for the cold season. Another name for the November full moon is the Frost Moon.

FESTIVAL FUN

5th November *Guy Fawkes or Bonfire Night*

"Remember, remember the 5th of November, Gunpowder, treason and plot!"

This is an annual commemoration of the day in 1605 when a man called Guy Fawkes was arrested for being a part of the 'Gunpowder Plot'. The plot was thought up by a group of men who wanted to blow up King James I and the Houses of Parliament in London. Guy Fawkes was found hiding beneath the House of Lords, guarding some explosives. Thankfully, the bombs never went off.

Nowadays, people spend the evening going to firework displays, standing around a big bonfire and eating hot dogs! It is a great way to chase away the winter blues.

11th November *Armistice Day (Remembrance Day)*

Armistice Day or Remembrance Day is a time for remembering all those who were killed in the First and Second World Wars and other wars that have since followed. A two-minute silence is held to remember the dead on the Sunday nearest to 11th November. People traditionally wear a red poppy around this time to show that they have not forgotten the

14th November *Diwali*

Diwali marks the start of the Hindu New Year. Sikhs and Jains also celebrate at this time. Diwali is five days long, and on the third day, many Hindus light special oil lamps called *diyas*. The lamps symbolise the triumph of light over darkness, good over evil, and knowledge over ignorance. Many gods – including Rama and his wife, Sita, and Lakshmi, the goddess of wealth and prosperity – are celebrated with music, *puja* (prayers), firework displays and by sharing traditional sweets.

22nd November *Stir-up Sunday*

This is the last Sunday before Advent, which is the period of time in which Christians prepare for Christmas, and is the day people traditionally make their Christmas puddings. In the old days, it was a time for families to get together to mix and steam the pudding. Everyone would take a turn to stir the pudding and make a special wish for the year ahead.

In some houses, silver coins are added to the pudding mix as finding a coin on Christmas Day is supposed to bring good luck.

29th November *First Sunday of Advent*

Advent lasts for four Sundays leading up to Christmas. Advent always begins on the Sunday that falls between 27th November and 3rd December. In churches, Christians light one candle every Sunday of Advent. It is common for people to also begin their own countdown to Christmas on 1st December with Advent calendars or Advent candles which have the numbers 1 to 24 on them.

REMEMBER, REMEMBER... HEDGEHOGS

★ If you are having a bonfire for Bonfire Night, it is best to pile up the leaves and wood on the actual day of bonfire. If you do it too far in advance, a hedgehog might think you have made a lovely place in which it can hibernate.

★ You can stop hedgehogs from finding their way into a bonfire pile by building a small fence with chicken wire around the edge. The wire should be about one metre high and should be held in place with bamboo sticks. Try to make the wire slope outwards – this will stop the hedgehogs from trying to climb in.

★ If you have already helped make a nice mound of garden waste to burn, perhaps you could move it to another place for the actual bonfire? This will give you a chance to look through the leaves and so on to make sure that there are no hedgehogs hiding inside the pile.

★ Just in case you have missed a hedgehog, make sure the adult in charge of the bonfire lights the pile on one side only and keeps away from the unlit side. That way, any hiding hedgehogs have a chance of escaping to safety.

TOP TIP

Never feed a hedgehog bread and milk! This can upset its tummy. In the wild, hedgehogs eat slugs and insects.

★ Finally, if you do find a hedgehog, put on some gardening gloves (or oven gloves) before touching its spiky little body. This is also to protect the hedgehog as they don't like getting the smell of humans on them!

★ Then, when you scoop up the creature, make sure you pick it up along with any leaves or bedding it has pulled around itself. Hedgehogs make cosy little nests, and you don't want to undo all their hard work.

★ Put the hedgehog, with its nest, in a high-sided cardboard box with plenty of newspaper or old towels. You'll need to put a lid on, too – remember to make some air holes in the lid so that the hedgehog can breathe.

★ Put the box in a quiet, safe place such as a shed or garage well away from noise. Once your bonfire is over, release the hedgehog into the wild again. Let it go under a hedge, bush or behind a stack of logs so that it feels safe.

DID YOU KNOW...

The number of hedgehogs in Britain is falling fast. To find out more about how to help hedgehogs, visit **www.britishhedgehogs.org.uk**

STARS OF THE EVENING

Have you ever been out for a walk, or on a long car journey, and seen a black mass of birds swooping and circling in the sky? If so, you have probably seen a 'murmuration' of starlings. It is the most amazing sight – like a swirling black cloud of birds that is constantly on the move. The birds perform incredible acrobatic stunts and the flock makes breath-taking patterns in the sky.

Murmurations become more common in November. More and more birds will flock together as the month goes on. Starlings choose places to roost together that are well sheltered from bad weather and predators. This means that they like woodlands, reed beds, cliffs and even disused buildings, too.

There are some beautiful places in Britain that have fantastic spots for watching murmurations: Gretna Green in Scotland and Brighton Pier are two of the more famous ones.

DID YOU KNOW...

The number of starlings roosting in one place can grow to as many as 750,000! They group together for safety, as predators such as hawks and peregrine falcons find it much harder to hunt down one bird in the middle of the huge hypnotising flocks. They also come together to keep warm at night and possibly to 'talk' to each other about where the best feeding areas are!

SEE THE SEALS

There are two types of seal found around the British coast: the common seal and the grey seal. The common seal gives birth to pups in the summer, whereas the grey seal has its babies in November. The grey seal spends a lot of time in the sea where it hunts for fish, squid, crab and lobster. They live in large family groups called 'colonies' which can be made up of thousands of seals.

★ The grey seal prefers the rocky coasts found in northern and western parts of the country and is most likely to be seen off the coast of Northumberland, Lincolnshire, the Orkney Islands and Cornwall.

★ The grey seal grows to a much larger size than the common seal and males are much bigger than females.

★ The grey seal has a much longer nose or 'snout' than the common seal and has nostrils spaced further apart!

★ Seals like to leave the water to rest and bask in the sun after they have been hunting.

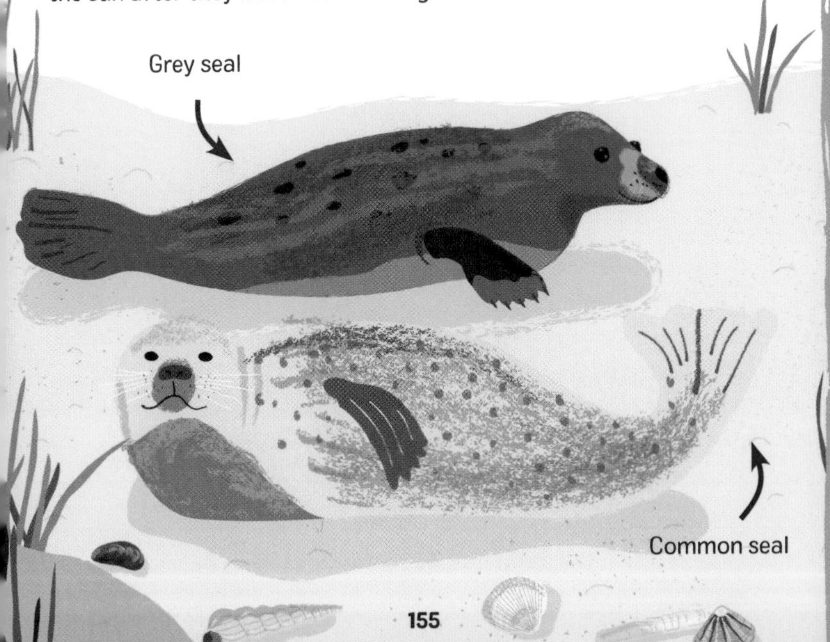

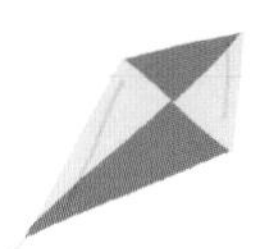

LET'S GO FLY A KITE

It can get quite windy in November – which means it's perfect weather for flying a kite! You don't need to spend money on an expensive one. Have a go at making your own recyclable kite from newspaper and wood.

You will need:

Sticks about 60 cm long
5 m string
Newspaper
Glue (a bottle with a nozzle for easy spreading is good)
1 m coloured ribbon

TOP TIP

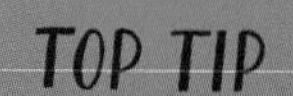

Make the kite on a rainy day – then wait for a bright, dry, windy day to try it out.

1. *Look for sticks in the park, garden or woods.*

2. *Use small pieces of string to tie the sticks into a cross – the horizontal stick will need to be slightly shorter than the vertical one.*

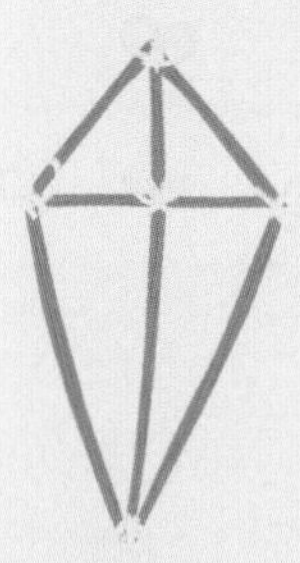

3. *Tie the string around the edge of the sticks to make a diamond shape. Don't cut the string until you have done this! (You might need to ask an adult to make small cuts or notches into the sticks to help the string stay in place.)*

4. *Unfold your newspaper and cut a pattern to match the shape of your kite frame. Make sure the paper is about 3–5 cm larger than your frame all the way around so that you can fold the edges over the string.*

5 *On a flat surface, lay out your paper with your stick-and-string frame on top, then fold the edges of your paper over the string.*

6 *Glue the paper into place.*

7 *Tie the longest piece of string you have to where the sticks cross. This is the string you'll hold on to when you fly your kite, so the longer the string, the higher the kite will fly!*

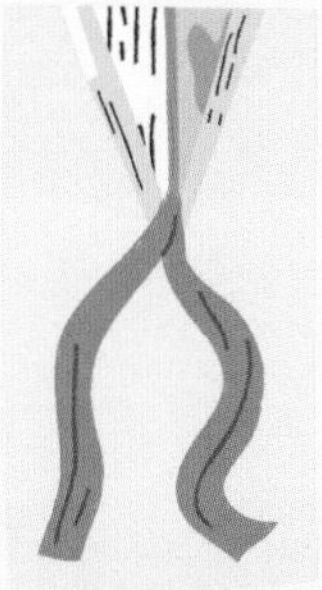

8 *To decorate your kite, tie a long ribbon (or ribbons!) to the longest point of the diamond. This is the tail of your kite.*

9 *Run outside on a windy day, take hold of the long string, run a little more, and . . . your kite will soar up into the sky like a paper bird!*

WILD WINTER WALKS

Sometimes winter walks can seem boring. The weather is not great and you are trudging along through mud, wishing you were tucked up snug indoors instead. A good idea to make walks more fun is to play games on your way. See if you can get the grown-ups to join in! You are bound to be faster than they are . . .

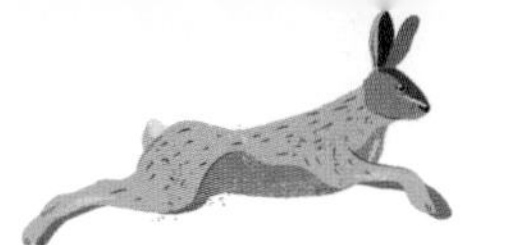

Foxes and Hares!

The best place to play this game is in the woods, as there will be plenty of places to hide. However, if your 'hares' are fast runners then you can play this anywhere as they will race off as soon as you shout, "Go!" The game is for a minimum of four players. You'll need two whistles and it's a good idea to wear sturdy trainers or running shoes. Before you start, decide on the end point – a particular bench or tree or rock, for example! The aim of the game is for the hares to reach that end point without being caught by the 'foxes'.

How to Play

★ Choose two people to be the hares. Give them a whistle. The rest of the players are the foxes.

★ Count to 100 slowly as the hares run off.

★ The leader blows a whistle to signal the start and the foxes race off after the hares.

★ From that point on, the hares must whistle every minute or so. This way the foxes can listen out for which direction the hares have run in.

★ The hares must try to outrun the foxes for as long as possible. They can hide if the foxes are catching up with them, but they must blow the whistle every minute to give the foxes clues as to where they are.

★ The hares try to reach the end point without getting caught.

★ If the foxes catch the hares, they should blow hard on their whistle to signal everyone to head back to the start area.

★ Then you can start the game all over again – if you are not too out of puff!

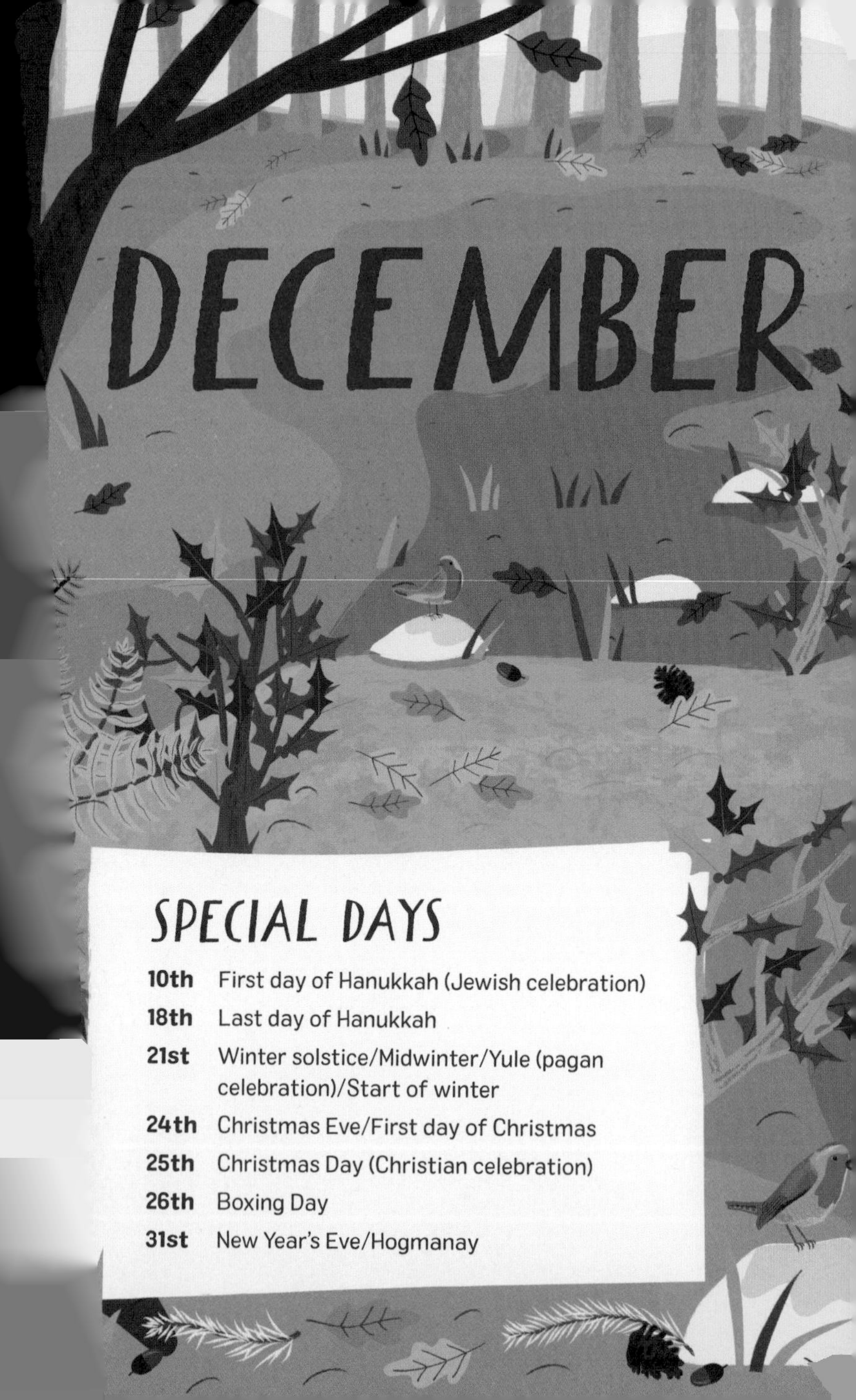

DECEMBER

SPECIAL DAYS

10th	First day of Hanukkah (Jewish celebration)
18th	Last day of Hanukkah
21st	Winter solstice/Midwinter/Yule (pagan celebration)/Start of winter
24th	Christmas Eve/First day of Christmas
25th	Christmas Day (Christian celebration)
26th	Boxing Day
31st	New Year's Eve/Hogmanay

ANNIVERSARIES

250 years ago . . .

On 17 December 1770, the German composer Ludwig van Beethoven was baptized. One of the most incredible things about him was that he wrote some of his best pieces of music after he had completely lost his hearing!

300 years ago . . .

On 31 December 1720, Charles Edward Stuart was born. He is best known as Bonnie Prince Charlie.

> *"Chill December brings the sleet,*
> *Blazing fire and Christmas treat."*
>
> SARA COLERIDGE (1802–1852)

In Britain, Christmas has become the main focus of this month. It is not the only festival going on, though. There are lots of other celebrations of light during this month because it contains the shortest day of the year. For many thousands of years, people have spent dark December thinking ahead to a time when the sun will come back. Whichever festival you celebrate, you are bound to have lots of fun, food and treats!

Why is December Called December?

This month gets its name from the Latin word for tenth, *decem*. The Anglo-Saxons called December *Ærra Geola* or the month 'before Yule'. Yule was an important winter festival and is still celebrated today by pagans. Many of the 'Yuletide' traditions have found their way into things we now think of as Christmas traditions.

The full moon this month is known as the Cold Moon or Long Night Moon.

WHATEVER THE WEATHER

December may be the start of winter, but by the end of the month the days are already getting lighter. It is because of this promise of longer, lighter days that the longest night has traditionally been a time for celebration. The dark can be sad or scary sometimes, but just think: if there was no darkness, there would be no light! This is what all the festivals this month are about: finding light in the darkness. The one thing you may hope for and not get this month is snow. You are far more likely to get snow from February through to March in Britain.

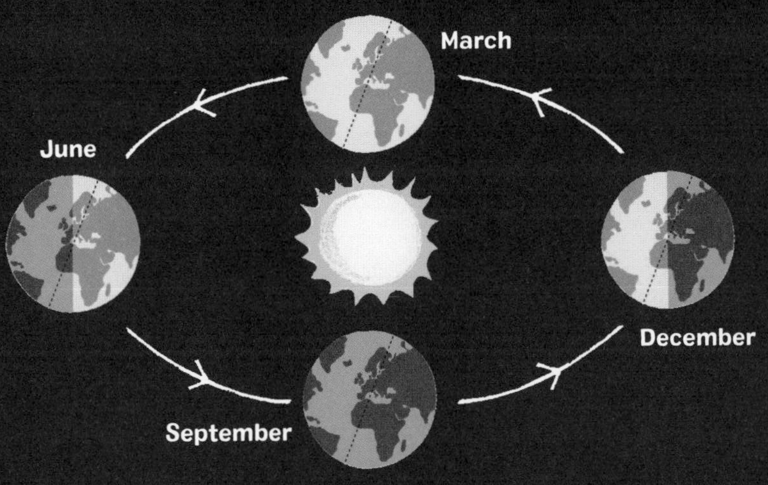

DID YOU KNOW...

Contrary to what people often think, the seasons don't change because of how far the Earth is from the sun. The change happens because the Earth goes around the sun at a tilted angle of about 23.4°. This causes different amounts of sunlight to reach the northern and southern hemispheres throughout the year. In fact, the Earth is closest to the sun a few weeks after the winter solstice.

FESTIVAL FUN

There's so much festival fun this month, you could be forgiven for thinking that December is one long celebration from start to finish!

21st December *Winter solstice or Midwinter or Yule*

The winter solstice or Midwinter falls on the shortest day of the year and has been celebrated in Britain for hundreds of years. Many pagan traditions of Yule have found their way into the celebration of Christmas. At Yule, pagans light candles and fires, decorate their homes with evergreen plants, feast, dance and give gifts. All these things are now traditional at Christmas, too.

Pagans also believe that hanging a sprig of holly near the door brings good luck and keeps away evil spirits. Mistletoe is also hung as a decoration and as a blessing and symbol of new life.

THE YULE LOG

The lighting of the Yule log is the most important part of the Yule festivities. Not only is it believed to conquer the darkness, it is thought to keep away evil spirits and bring good luck for the coming year. Years ago, the log had to be harvested from the householder's land or be given as a gift – it was not bought.

The Yule log would be placed in the fireplace and decorated with evergreen leaves, before cider or ale was poured on it and it was dusted with flour. Then it was lit with a piece of Yule log from the year before and the log would burn for 12 days. Then it was put out and a piece saved for the following year.

Five Ways to *Celebrate Midwinter*

★ Go on a walk to gather greenery for your home.
★ Light a fire or a circle of candles.
★ Tell stories around the fire or by candlelight.
★ Have a feast with your favourite food and favourite family and friends!
★ Write down a list of everything you have to be thankful for in the past year.

10th–18th December *Hanukkah*

Sometimes spelled *Chanukah*, this Jewish festival lasts for eight days. During this time, Jewish people remember how the Second Temple in Jerusalem was dedicated to God. Hanukkah is often called the festival of lights because the holiday is celebrated with the lighting of the *menorah* candlestick. Traditional foods are served, such as potato pancakes and jam-filled doughnuts called *sufganiyot*.

SLEIGH BELLS RING!

It is always fun to make some homemade Christmas decorations. It's a great thing to do at the beginning of the Christmas holidays when you are trying to pass the time, counting down to Christmas Day! If you pack them away carefully in January, these decorations will last for years and you can enjoy getting them out every December to put up around the house. If you don't want to make the whole scene, you could just make a few Santas. You could use them as place settings to show each family member where to sit at the table on Christmas Day.

Make a *Santa's Grotto*

This makes a lovely table decoration or you could put it on a windowsill or have it in your bedroom.

You will need:

Loo rolls/cardboard rolls from inside wrapping paper or paper towels etc
Red paper
Green paper
Brown paper
White paper
PVA glue
Pompoms in various colours
Pipe cleaners
Googly eyes
Cotton wool
Old shoebox
Pipe cleaners
Wrapping paper
Old matchboxes

How to Make Your Christmas Scene

1. *If you are using cardboard rolls instead of loo rolls, cut them to size. They should be about 10 cm high.*
2. *Cover the cardboard rolls in red paper for Santa, green for the elves, brown for the reindeer and white for the snowmen. Use glue to fix the paper in place.*
3. *Use the pompoms to make buttons and noses and use the pipe cleaners to make arms and antlers. You'll need a red pompom for Rudolf's nose!*
4. *Stick on googly eyes to finish the faces.*
5. *Use cotton wool for Santa's beard and the fur trim for his red coat. You can give the elves beards, too, if you like. Cotton wool can also be used to make your snowmen more snowy!*
6. *Cover the main box part of the shoe box in wrapping paper. This will be your sleigh.*
7. *Wrap the matchboxes, too, to make them look like presents, then put them in the sleigh.*
8. *Have fun setting up your scene with Santa sitting in the front of the sleigh and the reindeer out the front.*

TOP TIP

You could attach the reindeer to the sleigh with more pipe cleaners for reins.

FESTIVE HOUSES

You will see gingerbread houses everywhere at this time of year. They look so pretty and tempting to eat, too! They are very tricky to make, though, so why not make little house-shaped biscuits instead? They make lovely decorations to hang on the tree as well – as long as you don't eat them all the minute you've made them!

DID YOU KNOW...

In medieval times, the word 'gingerbread' just meant 'preserved ginger' and had nothing to do with the cakes and biscuits we think of today.

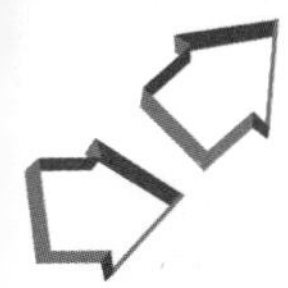

Recipe for *Gingerbread Houses*

Makes: 16 gingerbread biscuits

You will need:

Two baking trays
Greaseproof paper
Sieve
Medium bowl
Wooden spoon
House-shaped biscuit cutter
350 g plain flour
1 teaspoon of bicarbonate of soda
2 teaspoons of ground ginger
115 g butter, cubed
175 g soft light brown sugar
4 tablespoons of golden syrup
1 egg, beaten
Icing pens
Small sweets such as dolly mixtures

1. *Preheat the oven to 190°C/170°C fan/Gas Mark 5.*
2. *Lightly grease or line the baking trays.*
3. *Sieve the flour, bicarbonate of soda and ginger into the bowl.*
4. *Rub in the butter with your fingertips until it looks like large breadcrumbs, then stir in the sugar.*
5. *Beat the golden syrup into the egg with a wooden spoon, then stir into the flour mixture.*
6. *Knead the dough on a lightly floured work surface or large chopping board until it is smooth.*
7. *Roll out the dough until it is about ½ cm thick then use the biscuit cutter to make house shapes.*
8. *Bake the biscuits in the oven for about 10–12 minutes until they are golden and have puffed up slightly.*
9. *Let them sit on the tray for a few minutes before moving to a wire rack and allow them to cool completely.*
10. *Decorate the houses using different coloured icing pens and use icing to stick on the sweets for decoration, too.*

TOP TIP

To hang these on the tree, make a hole in the top of each biscuit roof before you bake them, then after baking, thread ribbon through the hole.

25th December *Christmas Day*

The word Christmas comes from the Anglo-Saxon word *Cristes Mæsse*. It is the Christian celebration of the birth of Jesus Christ. In fact, his birth date is unknown. However, Christians wanted a day to celebrate their belief that Jesus brought goodness and light into the world. As there were already 'light festivals' at this time of year such as Yule, it made sense to have Christmas then as well.

Saturnalia is an ancient Roman festival that probably influenced how and when Christmas is celebrated. It was dedicated to the god Saturn. All work and business stopped during the festival, and slaves were given a few days of freedom. People said *"Io Saturnalia!"* to each other the way people today might say "Happy Christmas!" or "Happy Hanukkah!" At the end of the festival people would make presents of candles to one another or wax models of fruit.

31st December *New Year's Eve or Hogmanay*

It is the last day of the year! Just before midnight it is traditional to turn on a radio or television to follow the countdown of the last few minutes of the old year and to watch the display of fireworks over the River Thames in London. At this point, people often hug and kiss and start to sing the song 'Auld Lang Syne' – although they often don't know the words! Here they are so that you can sing them this year:

"Should auld acquaintance be forgot
and never brought to mind?
Should auld acquaintance be forgot,
and auld lang syne?
For auld lang syne my dear,
For auld lang syne.
We'll tak'a cup o'kindness yet,
for auld lang syne."

The words were written by the Scottish poet Robert Burns in 1788. The song asks if it's right to forget old friends and things that have happened in the past.

DID YOU KNOW...

In England and Scotland, New Year's Day used to be 25th March. Scotland made 1st January New Year's Day in 1602 and England followed in 1751.

Just After Midnight...

In Scotland, New Year's Eve is known as Hogmanay. If you're lucky enough to be in Scotland on 1st January (and you're allowed to stay up on New Year's Eve until after midnight!) you might be able to join in with the tradition of First Footing.

The 'first foot' to come in through the front door after the last stroke of midnight is supposed to bring good luck. The 'first footer' should be carrying a piece of coal, some bread, salt and a small drink (known as a 'wee dram'). These items are thought to bring warmth, good food, long life and good cheer for the year ahead.

OUT IN THE WILD

While we humans are busy huddling by the fire and staying warm and cosy, nature carries on working. If you have had enough of being stuck indoors, get your family out on a nature walk. Wrap up warm and keep your eyes peeled. It might be winter, but there's still lots to see!

Robins are very busy at this time of year singing to protect their territories and finding food.

Listen out as the sun goes down and you might hear tawny owls calling to one another. The female calls out, "Too-wit," and the male answers her, "Too-whoo!"

Go for a walk around a river estuary. Birds flock to these places in the winter as the water does not freeze so there is always a lot of food to be found. You might even see a kingfisher or an otter.

Foxes are out hunting in the early evening. They can often be seen slinking into hedges or scurrying down driveways just after the sun has set.

Go for a walk by the sea. This is a great time of year to search the empty beaches for treasures – strange twisted lumps of driftwood, shells, pebbles and seed pods can all be used to make beautiful decorations.

Walk in the woods, too! Collect holly and ivy and pine cones and twigs and then come home and have fun making natural decorations for the house.

VISIT A LONELY NEIGHBOUR

Christmas is a lovely time to get together and share good things. It can be even more rewarding if you can find the time to do this with people you would not normally spend time with.

Do you know someone near you who might be lonely at this time of year? Perhaps you know an elderly neighbour who doesn't have family nearby? Why not ask a grown-up in your family if you can go round and pay a visit? Or ask if you could invite the neighbour round to your house for a cup of tea and one of your homemade gingerbread houses?

WRAPPING UP THE YEAR

"There is a time for everything, and a season for every activity under the heavens."

(ECCLESIASTES 3, FOUND IN THE HEBREW *TANAKH* AND THE *BIBLE*)

So, it's time to say goodbye to the old and make way for the new. Maybe you'll make those New Year's resolutions all over again . . . and just maybe you'll do better at keeping them in 2021! Whatever you do, and wherever you are, thank you for reading this book and

HAPPY NEW YEAR TO YOU AND YOUR FRIENDS AND FAMILY!

CALENDAR 2020

JANUARY

Mo	Tu	We	Th	Fr	Sa	Su
		1	2	3	4	5
6	7	8	9	10	11	12
13	14	15	16	17	18	19
20	21	22	23	24	25	26
27	28	29	30	31		

Phases of the Moon

3: ◐ 10: ○ 17: ◑ 24: ●

FEBRUARY

Mo	Tu	We	Th	Fr	Sa	Su
					1	2
3	4	5	6	7	8	9
10	11	12	13	14	15	16
17	18	19	20	21	22	23
24	25	26	27	28	29	

Phases of the Moon

2: ◐ 9: ○ 23: ◑ 15: ●

MARCH

Mo	Tu	We	Th	Fr	Sa	Su
						1
2	3	4	5	6	7	8
9	10	11	12	13	14	15
16	17	18	19	20	21	22
23	24	25	26	27	28	29
30	31					

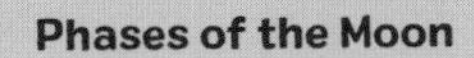

Phases of the Moon

2: 9: 16: 24:

APRIL

Mo	Tu	We	Th	Fr	Sa	Su
		1	2	3	4	5
6	7	8	9	10	11	12
13	14	15	16	17	18	19
20	21	22	23	24	25	26
27	28	29	30			

Phases of the Moon

1: 8: 14: 23: 30:

Mo	Tu	We	Th	Fr	Sa	Su
				1	2	3
4	5	6	7	8	9	10
11	12	13	14	15	16	17
18	19	20	21	22	23	24
25	26	27	28	29	30	31

Phases of the Moon

30: 7: 14: 22:

Mo	Tu	We	Th	Fr	Sa	Su
1	2	3	4	5	6	7
8	9	10	11	12	13	14
15	16	17	18	19	20	21
22	23	24	25	26	27	28
29	30					

Phases of the Moon

28: 5: 13: 21:

JULY

Mo	Tu	We	Th	Fr	Sa	Su
		1	2	3	4	5
6	7	8	9	10	11	12
13	14	15	16	17	18	19
20	21	22	23	24	25	26
27	28	29	30	31		

Phases of the Moon

27: 5: 12: 20:

AUGUST

Mo	Tu	We	Th	Fr	Sa	Su
					1	2
3	4	5	6	7	8	9
10	11	12	13	14	15	16
17	18	19	20	21	22	23
24	25	26	27	28	29	30

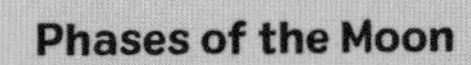

Phases of the Moon

25: 3: 11: 19:

SEPTEMBER

Mo	Tu	We	Th	Fr	Sa	Su
	1	2	3	4	5	6
7	8	9	10	11	12	13
14	15	16	17	18	19	20
21	22	23	24	25	26	27
28	29	30				

Phases of the Moon

24: 2: 10: 17:

OCTOBER

Mo	Tu	We	Th	Fr	Sa	Su
			1	2	3	4
5	6	7	8	9	10	11
12	13	14	15	16	17	18
19	20	21	22	23	24	25
26	27	28	29	30	31	

Phases of the Moon

23: 1: 10: 16:

Mo	Tu	We	Th	Fr	Sa	Su
						1
2	3	4	5	6	7	8
9	10	11	12	13	14	15
16	17	18	19	20	21	22
23	24	25	26	27	28	29

Phases of the Moon

22: ◐ 30: ○ 8: ◑ 15: ●

DECEMBER

Mo	Tu	We	Th	Fr	Sa	Su
	1	2	3	4	5	6
7	8	9	10	11	12	13
14	15	16	17	18	19	20
21	22	23	24	25	26	27
28	29	30	31			

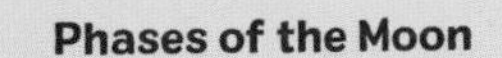

◐ 30: ○ 8: ◑ 14: ●

NOTES

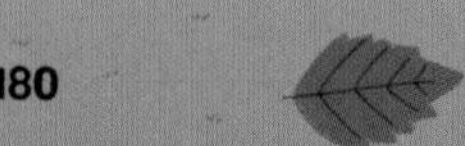

GLOSSARY

Advent The period leading up to Christmas

All Saints' Eve A Christian festival to remember saints and loved ones who have died

Allah The name of God for Muslims and Arab Christians

Anglo-Saxons People who lived in Great Britain from 410 until 1066

Apple Day A celebration of apples and orchards

April Fool's Day The first day of April, when people play jokes on each other

Ascension Day A Christian holy day to celebrate the day Jesus rose into heaven

Ash Wednesday The beginning of Lent

Beltane An ancient pagan festival that celebrates the return of summer

Bible The Christian holy book

Birthday Honours The titles given to people on the Queen's official birthday

Birth flower A flower linked to the month of a person's birth

Birthstone A gemstone linked to the month of a person's birth

Blue moon A second full moon in a calendar month

Buddhist Someone who believes in and follows the teachings of the Buddha

Burns Night A celebration of the Scottish poet Robert Burns

Candlemas A Christian festival celebrating the first time that baby Jesus was taken to the temple

Catholic Someone who follows a branch of Christianity led by the Pope

Chinese New Year A colourful celebration of the start of the Chinese year, also known as the 'Spring Festival'

Christian Someone who follows the religion of Christianity and believes in God, Jesus Christ and the teachings of the *Bible*

Church The Christian place of worship

Crop circle A pattern made by flattening crops in a field, usually done overnight

Diwali A Hindu festival of lights to celebrate the victory of light over darkness

Easter A Christian festival to remember the death and return to life of Jesus Christ

Eid al-Adha Also known as the 'Sacrifice Feast', this Islamic festival honours Ibrahim's willingness to obey Allah and marks the end of the *Hajj* pilgrimage to Mecca

Eid al-Fitr Also known as the 'Festival of the Breaking of the Fast', this Islamic festival is a three-day celebration to mark the end of Ramadan

Equator An imaginary line drawn around the middle of the Earth at an equal distance from the north and south poles

Epiphany A Christian holy day, held in January, which marks the end of the Christmas period

Equinox The time twice a year when the length of day and night is exactly equal

Eta Aquariids A meteor shower formed by particles of dust left behind by Halley's Comet

Fast To spend a period of time without eating or drinking

Fertility The ability to create children or young

First Footing A Scottish New Year's tradition, where the 'first footer' is the first person to walk through the door after midnight

First quarter One quarter of the way through the moon's cycle, when we can see exactly half of the moon's face

Full moon When the entire face of the moon is lit up by the sun's rays

Ganesh Chaturthi A 10-day Hindu festival to worship the god Ganesha

Gemstone A precious or semi-precious stone

Gleaning Gathering leftover grain after a harvest

Guy Fawkes A member of a group of English Catholics who tried to assassinate King James in 1604 by blowing up the Houses of Parliament

Hanukkah An eight-day 'festival of lights' celebrated by Jewish people, to remember how the Jewish army freed Jerusalem and took back the temple, which they re-dedicated to God

Harvest Gathering crops

Hemisphere Half of the Earth, divided into northern and southern hemispheres by the equator

Hibernate When an animal or plant goes to sleep for the winter

Hindu Someone who follows the South Asian religion of Hinduism, involving the belief in reincarnation and the worship of many gods

Hogmanay The Scottish word for the last day of the year

Holi A Hindu spring festival in celebration of the god Krishna

Holy Spirit Christians believe God exists in three forms at the same time, as God in heaven, as Jesus Christ in heaven, and as the Holy Spirit, which is everywhere

Imbolc A pagan festival marking the beginning of spring

Isra and Mi'raj An Islamic celebration of the Prophet Muhammad's journey from Mecca to Jerusalem and his journey into heaven, when Allah revealed to Muhammad that Muslims should pray five times a day

Jain Someone who follows the ancient Indian religion of Jainism that teaches *ahimsa* (non-violence) to all living creatures

Jerusalem The capital city of Israel, believed to be holy by Jews, Christians and Muslims

Jew Someone who follows the religion of Judaism and believes in God, the Hebrew prophets and the teachings of the *Torah*

Lammas A pagan celebration of the first harvest

Last quarter Three quarters of the way through the moon's cycle, when we can see exactly half of the moon's face

Leap year A year with 366 days in it, which occurs once every four years

Lent A Christian period of fasting in the run-up to Easter

Litha The Anglo-Saxon word for midsummer

Lohri A Punjabi midwinter festival celebrated by Sikhs and Hindus

Lughnasadh A Gaelic festival celebrating the beginning of the harvest season

Maia The Greek goddess of fertility

Matzo A flatbread that Jewish people eat at Passover

May Day The first day of May, celebrated by dancing and singing

Mecca The holiest city of Islam

Meteor A fiery streak in the sky, created when dust and rocks from the tail of a comet pass through the Earth's atmosphere

Michaelmas A Christian festival held at the end of September to honour the angels

Midsummer The longest day and the shortest night of the year, also known as the summer solstice

Midwinter The shortest day and the longest night of the year, also known as the winter solstice

Migrate To move from one place to another

Morris dancing A form of English folk dance with music

Mosque The Islamic place of worship

Muhammad The Muslim Prophet and founder of Islam

Murmuration When hundreds or thousands of starlings fly together in a flowing pattern

Muslim Someone who follows the religion of Islam and believes in Allah, the Prophet Muhammad, the five pillars of Islam and the teachings of the *Qur'an*

Neap tide A tide that happens twice a month, when the difference between high tide and low tide is at its lowest

New moon The first phase in the moon's cycle, when just a very thin crescent shape is visible at night

Old Testament The first part of the *Bible*, originally written in Hebrew

Ostara A pagan festival which is celebrated at the spring equinox

Pagan A follower of paganism, a pre-Christian religion, who believes in many gods and goddesses

Passover A Jewish celebration to remember how Moses helped the Israelites escape from Egypt

Pentecost A Christian festival on the seventh Sunday after Easter, to celebrate the day after his death when Jesus returned to his disciples in the form of the Holy Spirit

Promised Land The land that Jewish people believe was given by God to Abraham and his descendants

Purification The process of making something or someone clean

Purim A Jewish holiday in memory of when the Jewish people were saved from a cruel man called Haman

Qur'an The Islamic holy book

Raksha Bandhan A Hindu festival that celebrates the relationship between brothers and sisters

Ramadan A month when Muslims hold a fast during the hours of daylight to become closer to Allah, and to remember the time that the Qur'an was first revealed to the Prophet Muhammad

Resolution A decision to do, or not do something

Samhain Eve A pagan festival for giving thanks at the end of the harvest

Sea Sunday The day when Christians pray for sailors and their families

Seder A special Jewish feast to celebrate the beginning of Passover

Shavuot A Jewish holiday to remember the day that God gave Moses the Torah

Shrove Tuesday The day before the Christian period of fasting called Lent begins, also known as 'Pancake Day'

Sikh Someone who follows the religion of Sikhism and believes in the writings and teachings of the Ten Sikh Gurus

Spring tide A tide just after a new or full moon, when the difference between high tide and low tide is at its highest

Swan Upping An annual ceremony in which mute swans are taken from the River Thames to be counted and marked to identify them, before being released

Synagogue The Jewish place of worship

Ten Commandments A list of laws or rules that Christians and Jews follow that they believe were given by God to Moses

Tide The rising and falling of the sea

Torah The Jewish holy book

Trooping the colour A ceremony performed to celebrate the Queen's birthday

Tu B'Shevat Jewish New Year, also known as the 'New Year for Trees'

Twelfth Night A festival some Christians celebrate to mark the coming of the Epiphany

Wassailing A pagan tradition of blessing the apple trees in the new year

Whitsun Another name for the Christian festival of Pentecost

Yom Kippur A Jewish holiday for saying sorry for things you have done wrong and asking for forgiveness

Yule A pagan festival held in midwinter to celebrate the winter solstice

INDEX

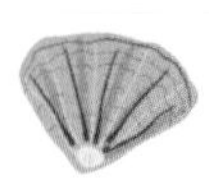

Advent 146, 151, 186
Albert Einstein 49
All Saints' Day 146
All Saints' Eve/All Hallows' Eve 132, 137, 186
All Souls' Day 146
Allah 39, 186, 187, 188, 189
Andromeda 79
Anemone 115
Animal prints 129
Anne Brontë 7
Anne Frank 35
Apollo 52
Apple-bobbing 137
Apple day 132, 140, 186
April Fool's Day 48, 53, 186
Armistice Day 146, 150
Ascension Day 62, 186
Ash Wednesday 20, 25, 186
Augustus 106
Aquarius 23
Auld Lang Syne 170
Autumn equinox 118
Badger 14, 15, 33, 72, 129
Banded demoiselle damselfly 70
Bank holidays
  May 62
  Spring 62
  Summer (England, Northern Ireland and Wales) 104
  Summer (Scotland) 104
Battle of Britain 91
Beaver 149
Beltane 62, 66, 67, 186
Bewick's swans 142, 143
Bible 81, 173, 186, 188
Big Garden Birdwatch 16
Bilberries 117
Birth flower 81, 106, 186
Birthday honours 80, 186
Birthstone 81, 106, 186
Blackberries 117
Blackbird 16
Blackcap 43
Blenny 115
Blitz 119
Blue Moon 51, 186
Blue tit 16
Bob Marley 21
Bonfire 150, 152, 153
Boxing Day 160
Brandt's bat 73
Brown long-eared bat 73
Buck Moon/Thunder Moon/Hay Moon/Wort Moon 93
Buddha 186
Bug hotel 74, 75
Bugs Bunny 91
Burns Night 6, 186
Butterfish 115
Butterflies 42, 81, 86, 87
  Brown argus 87
  Clouded yellow 87
  Comma 87
  Common blue 87
  Green-veined white 87
  Holly blue 87
  Large white/Cabbage white 87
  Male brimstone 87
  Orange-tip 87
  Painted lady 87
  Red admiral 87
Camping 88, 89
Candlemas 20, 24, 186
Canis Major/Great Dog 28
Canon Hardwicke Rawnsley 7
Cassiopeia 79, 109
Caterpillar hunt 86
Centaur 149
Chaffinch 43
Charles Dickens 77
Charles Edward Stuart (Bonnie Prince Charles) 161
Chiffchaff 43
Chinese New Year (Year of the Rat) 6, 12, 186
Chopsticks 13
Christmas 32, 89, 151, 160, 162, 164, 166, 167, 170, 173, 186, 187
Cloud formations 27
  Alto 27
  Cirrus/Cirro 27
  Cumulonimbus 27, 50
  Cumulus/Cumulo 27
  Nimbus/Nimbo 27
  Stratus/Strato 27
Coal tit 16
Cold Moon/Long Night Moon 162
Common frog 33
Common pipistrelle bat 73
Common seal 155
Conkers 124
Constellation viewer 108
Constellations 28, 52, 79, 107, 148
Crop circles 102, 186
Cuckoo 61, 83, 116
Cygnus 109, 121
Daffodils 14, 15, 41
Dam 149
Daylight saving 34, 36, 132, 145
Decorating eggs 56
Deer 93, 129
Diwali 146, 186
Dog 60, 129
Dormouse 42
Dragonflies 47, 70
Duck 70, 129
Earth 28, 29, 37, 51, 65, 92, 102, 110, 135, 163, 187, 188, 189
Easter eggs 54, 56
Easter 41, 48, 54, 56, 67, 186
Eid al-Adha 90, 186
Eid al-Fitr 62, 67, 186
Elderberries 117
Epiphany 6, 10, 187, 189
Eta Equariids 65
Father's Day 76
Feast of the Three Kings 10
Februa 22
Ferdinand Magellan 147
Fireworks 150
First footing 6, 171, 187
Florence Nightingale 63
Flower Moon 65
Fox 14, 15, 33, 72, 129, 159, 172
Foxes and hares game 159
Foxgloves 70
Frogs 33, 75
Gabriel 39
Gajak 10
Gemini 65
Ganesh Chaturthi 104, 111, 187
Ganesha 111, 187
Glastonbury Festival 119
Goby 115
God 39, 67, 81, 165, 186, 187, 188, 189
Goldfinch 16
Great-crested newt 33
Great tit 16, 45
Green Man 66
Green shore crab 115
Grey heron 71

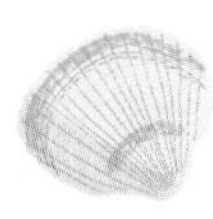

Grey seal 155
Growing plants
Carrots 57
Dahlia 57
Geraniums 57
Lavender 57
Nasturtiums 57
Radishes 57
Runner beans 57
Strawberries 57
Sunflowers 57
Sweet peas 57
Watercress 57
Gurh 10
Guy Fawkes Night 146, 150, 187
Halley's comet 65, 187
Halloween 132, 137, 138
Hanukah 160, 165, 170, 187
Harvest Moon/Corn Moon 129
Harvest time 126
Hawks 154
Hazel catkins 14, 15
Hedgehogs 42, 72, 73, 129, 153
Hercules 52
Hibernation 152, 154, 187
Holi 34, 38, 187
Homemade paper 69
Honeysuckle 81
Horse chestnut tree 124
Horseshoe bat 73
House martin 61
House sparrow 16, 45
Hunter's Moon/ Blood Moon 135
Hydra 52
Ibrahim 186
Igloo 30
Imbolc 20, 24, 187
Isra and Mi'raj 34, 39, 187
J. J. Thomson 105
Janus 8, 9
Jesus Christ 24, 25, 39, 54, 67, 94, 170, 186, 187, 188
John Barleycorn 110
John Lennon 133
John Logie Baird 133
John Tenniel 21
Joseph Barbera 21
Julius Ceasar 29, 93, 94, 106
Juno 79
Jupiter 28, 79
Kingfisher 46, 172
Kite 156, 157
Krishna 187
Lakshmi 151
Lammas 104, 110, 112, 113, 188
Lapwing 43
Last Supper 54
Leap Year 29, 188
Lent 22, 25, 37, 41, 186, 188, 189
Leo 109
Lewis Carroll 21
Libra 121
Lily 12
Lohri 6, 10, 188
Long-tailed tit 16
Ludwig van Beethoven 161
Lugh/Lug 110
Lughnasadh 104, 110, 188
Mabon/Harvest Festival 118, 122
Magpie 16
Maia 64, 188
Mallard ducks 70
Mars 28
Marsh tit 45
Martinmas 146
Matzo 54, 188
Maundy Thursday 54
May Day 62, 66, 188
Mayflower, The 119
Maypole 66
Menorah 165
Mercury 28
Meteor shower 65, 187
Michaelmas 118, 123, 188
Midsummer 76, 78, 82, 188
Midwinter 6, 160, 164, 165, 188, 189
Migration 33, 142, 188
Moon, The 18, 22, 27, 28, 37, 38, 39, 51, 55, 65, 67, 78, 79, 93, 102, 107, 110, 111, 129, 135, 149, 162, 186, 187, 188, 189
Morris dancing 83, 188
Moses 39, 54, 81, 188, 189
Moths
Angle shades116
Antler moth 116
Burnished brass 116
Garden tiger 116
Green carpet 116
Large yellow underwing 116
Ruby tiger 116
Setaceous Hebrew character 116
Mother Teresa 105
Mother's Day 34, 41
Muhammad 39, 187, 188, 189
Muharram 104, 111
National Trust 7
Nature notebook 15, 47, 68, 70, 115
Neptune 28
Nest box 44, 45
Nettle picking 58
New Year's Day 6
New Year's Eve/ Hogmanay 160, 170, 171, 173
New Year's resolutions 9, 122, 173, 189
Notting Hill Carnival 104
Octavia Hill 7
Olympic ring game 98
Olympics 29, 90
Orion 28
Ostara 22, 34, 39, 40, 188
Otter 129, 172
Owl 14, 33, 172
Palmate newt 33
Paralympic Games 114
Park run 60
Passover 48, 54, 81, 188, 189
Pegasus 107
Pentecost/Whitsun 62, 67, 188, 189
Peregrine falcon 154
Perseus 109
Phases of the Moon 18, 37, 51, 79, 93, 112, 129, 135, 162, 174, 175, 176, 177, 178, 179
Pink Moon 51
Pipefish 115
Pisces 23, 109
Pond dipping 47
Poohsticks 19

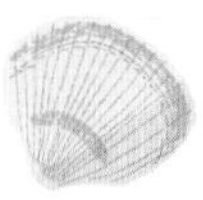

Pope 186
Porcelain crab 115
Poseidon 79
Press flowers 68
Primroses 14, 15
Prophet's Birthday 132, 136
Pumpkin carving 138, 139
Purim 34, 38, 189
Purnima 38
Queen's Official Birthday 76, 80, 186, 189
Qur'an 136, 186, 189
Rabbit 129
Raksha Bandhan 104, 110, 189
Rama 151
Ramadan 48, 55, 62, 67
Raspberries 100
Recipes
- Baked apples 141
- Blackberry and apple cake 117
- Blueberry pancakes 26
- Buttermilk bread for Lammas 112
- Easy strawberry jam 85
- Fat cakes 31
- Gingerbread houses 169
- Gorgeous courgette cake 127
- Homemade lemonade 101
- Nettle soup 59
- Ostara buns 40
- S'mores 89
- Sesame noodles 13
- Twelfth Night cake 11

River clean-up 103
Robert Burns 171, 186
Robert Hunter, Sir 7
Robin 16, 172
Rock pooling 115
Rosh Hashanah 118, 122
RSPB 16
Sagittarius 149
Samhain Ever 132, 136, 189
Sand martin 43
Sandpiper 19
Santa's grotto decorations 167
Sandwich tern 43
Saturn 28, 170
Saturnalia 170
Sea swimming 125
Sea shells
- Augur shell 95
- Banded Wedge shell 95
- Cockle 95
- Common limpet 95
- Common mussel 95
- Crab shell 95
- Dog whelk 95
- Oyster 95
- Razor shell 95
- Periwinkle 95
- Sea potato 95
- Shark's tooth 95
- Slipper limpet 95

Seashell grotto 94, 95
Sea Sunday 90, 189
Seals 155
Seder 54, 189
Shavuot 76, 81, 189
Shrimp 115
Shrove Tuesday (Pancake Day) 20, 25, 189
Sirius 28
Sita 151
Skimming stones 71
Skylark 43
Smooth newt 33
Snow angels 32
Snow lanterns 32
Snowdrops 14, 15
Solar System, The 28
Spiders 130–131
- Black lace weaver 131
- Cave spider 131
- False widow 131
- Garden spider 131
- House spider 131
- Lace webbed spider 131
- Money spider 131

Sponge 115
Spring equinox 34, 37, 39, 66, 187, 188
Squirrel 15, 129
St Andrew's Day 146
St David's Day 34
St George's Day 48
St James's Day/ Grotto Day 90, 94, 95
St Nicholas's Day 10
St Patrick's Day 34
St Piran's Day 34
St Swithun's Day 90, 94
St Valentine's Day 20, 25
Stargazing 18, 33
Starlings 154, 188
Stir-up Sunday 146, 151
Stonehenge 82, 102
Strawberry picking 84
Sufganiyot 165
Summer solstice 66, 76, 82, 188
Sun 14, 28, 29, 37, 50, 51, 55, 66, 72, 78, 82, 83, 92, 145, 155, 162, 163, 172, 187
Surya 10
Swallow 61
Swan upping 103, 189
Swift 45, 61
Tanakh 173
Taurus 65, 148
Tides 115, 125, 188, 189
Toads 33, 75, 145
- Common toad 33
- Natterjack toad 33

Toad Patrol 33
Torah 81, 189
Tortoise 42
Tree sparrow 45
Trick or treating 138
Trooping of the Colour 76, 80, 189
Tu B'Shevat (Jewish New Year) 20, 189
Twelfth Night 6, 10, 189
Uranus 28
VE Day 63
Venus 28, 51
Virgo 121
Wassailing 6, 10, 189
Water lilies 70
Wheatear 43
Whitstable Oyster Festival 94
Wildflowers
- Borage 70
- Broom 70
- Buttercups 70
- Common parsley 70
- Cow parsley 70
- Hawthorn 64, 70
- Ox-eye daisy 70
- Ragged robin 70
- Red campion 70

William Hanna 21
William Shakespeare 48
William Willett 144
William Wordsworth 49
Winston Churchill 77
Winter solstice 160, 163, 188, 189
Wood pigeon 16, 61
Wren 16
Yom kippur 118, 123, 189
Yule 160, 162, 164, 165, 170, 189
Zeus 97